LOVING YOUR NEIGHBOR

LOVING YOUR NEIGHBOR
A practical guide.

Steve Fales

Praeter Advisory, Weston

Praeter Advisory, Weston 33326

©2020 by Steven H. Fales

Published 2020

ISBN 978-1-7331446-2-9

*To all who heard the answer
to the lawyer's question,
and strive to fulfill it.*

Special Acknowledgment

Everything about this book was significantly improved by my friend Summer Gray, who read multiple versions of the manuscript, spent countless hours on the phone with me editing and discussing, and gave freely of her wisdom and expertise. My appreciation cannot be overstated.

Acknowledgments

It takes many people to bring a book to fruition. Here are a few who contributed heavily to this one:

- Debbie, for reading and copy editing the final manuscript, the final final manuscript, and the final final final manuscript, as well as invaluable fact-checking, plus helping navigate the maze of permissions, citations, notes, bibliography, and more.

- Luis, who allowed me to use his amazing story.

- Hayme, who interviewed Luis (since I can't speak Spanish) and whose enthusiasm about my writing was encouraging.

- Charlie, for the interior layout and a creative cover design.

- Sash, Jennifer, and Larry, mentors who taught me so much.

- Buddy and Becky; and Chad and Rachel, whose practical displays of love provided examples used in the book.

- Melinda, for always responding to my punctuation questions with a smile that was noticeable even via email.

- Linda (my wife), who has lived out every principle in this book in our relationship for more than four decades.

- And all those who have loved me, their neighbor, as they love themselves.

Foreword

Who is qualified to write a book about loving others? Someone who has thought deeply about what love looks like in everyday life and has the gift of communicating practical ways to go about it. Someone who has attempted it, however imperfectly, and continues to. Someone who has the courage and conviction to show up for others consistently. Someone like the author, Steve Fales.

I first met Steve in 1982. I had recently moved home from college with a degree in English and an old blue Volvo full of books. I found myself missing the intellectual stimulation of the academic world. One Tuesday night, my sister attended a Bible study at Steve's house, and I tagged along. During the group discussion, I mentioned the classic novel *Crime and Punishment*. Coincidentally, Steve had recently finished reading it, and, like me, had been powerfully impacted. That simple connection began a lifelong friendship.

For the past 38 years, Steve has had a profound effect on me as well as on my family. A life-long learner, teacher, mentor, and someone who is willing to look beneath the surface, Steve does not shy away from those lonely areas of pain we all harbor. He even ventures further, allowing others' pain to touch his own life.

Steve became a friend to my father, a quiet, intellectual man who did not easily open himself to others. But as he battled cancer, my father told me he always felt better after his frequent conversations with Steve. When my father became a Christian, Steve baptized him in the Atlantic Ocean one chilly morning. And when he died, Steve spoke at my father's funeral.

Steve came to our weddings too, walking my sister down the aisle in our father's place, and traveling to Atlanta to perform my marriage ceremony three years later. He hired my recently-widowed mother to work for his advertising agency part time.

Steve has a history of seeing others and, perhaps more importantly, a history of showing up. He is willing to be vulnerable, to talk honestly about his own struggles and journey in life. Because he has questioned and grown and changed, he offers safety to others.

In addition to the people I know about, I imagine there are numerous others whom Steve has quietly befriended. He has noticed them, listened to their stories, shown curiosity, shared his wisdom and skills, lovingly confronted, and made allowances for them; in other words, everything that this book encourages us to do to love another. These individuals may remain invisible to the world, but Steve has taken the time to see them. And being seen changes everything.

A lot has changed in my life since 1982. I returned to school and earned a master's degree, becoming a Licensed Professional Counselor, in the early 90s. As a therapist, I sit with hurting, often deeply wounded individuals and see firsthand the damage that a human being suffers when he or she has not been loved well. I listen to heartbreaking stories of loneliness and trauma, witnessing the healing that happens when someone feels seen and cared for. One person can make a tremendous difference in another's life.

Here is a book that unpacks how to make that difference. Steve Fales has written a helpful exploration of an important subject. I highly recommend that you read *Loving Your Neighbor: A practical guide*, because it will help prepare you to carry out one of life's highest and best callings.

Summer Gray, MS, LPC
September 2020

Contents

Introduction

*There is a voice inside which speaks
and says, "This is the real me!"*
– William James

Dan and Jeremy are on the same bowling team. Just about every Thursday night for the past four years they've seen each other at the lanes. They laugh, have some greasy pizza, and knock over a few pins. Both men would say they're pretty good friends.

For roughly five weeks, though, Jeremy didn't show up, and Dan didn't have the slightest idea why. No one else on the team did either. Then, just like that, he was back. "Where you been, my man?" Dan asked. "On the dark side of the moon," came the reply. What Jeremy didn't say was that he had spent the last month in a hotel two time zones away. He and his wife were sticking close to the facility where their daughter was in treatment for an eating disorder. Group therapy for parents was every other day. The $38,000 price tag required a second mortgage on the house, but you do anything for your kids.

The team lost their game that night, though not by much.

Julia has a storybook life. At least according to her social media. A handsome boyfriend. Trendy dinners out. Elaborate weekends. And all smiles. Many of her 648 connections feel envious.

So it sent quite a shockwave through the online community when someone in the loop posted, "OMG! Saw Julia last night. She had a black eye. I think her bf hit her."

Julia has since changed her profile picture to a shot of her cat.

Frank's kind of a quiet guy at the office. He comes in, does his job without saying much, and goes home. The home to which he goes, however, is anything but typical. It's a small 1,500 square foot ranch style—nothing special about that—but with an eight-car garage out back.

That's because Frank restores classic Corvettes. In fact, he just sold a beautiful 1963 split window for over six figures. He used the money to refurbish a basketball court in the inner city neighborhood where he grew up. Somehow, Frank escaped the gang life of his teen years and is doing well for himself now.

— — — — — — — — — —

Situations like these are too common. The world is full of people who are partially invisible, yet as unique as their DNA. They have stories full of pain, struggles, and sometimes grand victories, but they live behind masks, hiding their real selves.

People crave an opportunity to tell their stories. Finding someone who will listen and ask questions, though, is extremely difficult. Rarer still are those who pay close enough attention to notice the needs of men and women around them. Some people genuinely want to make a difference, but it's tough to know how.

"Let me know if there's anything I can do to help," they say, but seldom does anyone follow up. Such a strange dilemma.

It doesn't make it any easier that some people rub us the wrong way. They have quirks we find annoying. It's not that they cross obvious ethical or legal lines. They're simply hard to be around.

True connection is so scarce that the ones who do have the skills can wind up running in circles, working hard to help a long list of people who don't give back—because they can't. They're emotionally bankrupt and just looking for help. It's like trying to put out a fire with a thimble.

— — — — — — — — — —

There is a solution. People must learn how to love others, and love themselves at the same time. Not how to navigate starry-eyed, romantic love, but how to express love in everyday interactions. The love that can be sensed by another person and makes him or her feel cared for. The love that is displayed practically.

This book is about just that. It's a journey into the dynamic world of one of the greatest endeavors a human can undertake: learning to love others in ways that are meaningful.

So, on behalf of all the bowling buddies, social media acquaintances, and unassuming co-workers out there, thank you for joining this study. You're about to explore how to make a loving difference in people's lives. Nothing could be better.

PART ONE

Why Do We Need A Book
About Loving Our Neighbor?

1

Priority One

Now these three remain: faith, hope, and love.
But the greatest of these is love.

– Saint Paul

Life's deepest messages sometimes come to us in surprising ways. That happened to me one morning as I was out for a run in New York City.

On that particular day I had the privilege of crossing the Williamsburg Bridge, which connects the Lower East Side to Brooklyn. It's a concrete walkway high in the sky, over vehicles and trains, used by pedestrians, runners, and bicyclists. Apparently, it has been discovered by street artists as well.

I was enjoying the experience, aware of what the exertion was doing to my body, and letting my mind wander as occurs so naturally while running. Looking near my feet I saw the word "Love," written in graffiti. A few steps later, was the word "Is." Soon after, "Always." I then realized that this was a message, given one word at a time so it unfolded as a person moved along. The full message read:

Love
Is
Always
The
Appropriate
Response.

Love is always the appropriate response. I've read that sentiment many times on onion skin paper with gold edges, inside a leather-bound holy book believed to be divinely inspired. Here, on bare concrete, in ordinary spray paint, put there by who-knows-who was the same spiritual truth.

Simon & Garfunkel, in the song, "The Sounds Of Silence," told us that prophets' words often appear in the most unlikely places. No doubt the prophets have been to Williamsburg Bridge.

— — — — — — — — — —

The Search For What's Important

There he is. Jesus of Nazareth. We see him in the center of a crowd—speaking, teaching, answering questions. His responses contain wisdom, spoken with authority. Many people even believe he is the son of God.

A few of Jesus' adversaries are there too. They shout out a trick question or a philosophical riddle now and then, hoping to stump him. But he handles even the toughest ones with calm precision. The opposition remains frustrated.

Suddenly a lawyer makes his way to the front, eager to speak. He has a request guaranteed to put Jesus in an awkward position and turn public opinion against him.

"Teacher," he asks, "which command in the law is the greatest?"

Everyone's eyes are fixed on the young, popular rabbi. Which commandment will he say is the most important?

Who do you see in the gathering? Certainly there are many senior citizens there. They listen with anticipation. They want Jesus to say that the greatest commandment is, "Honor your father and mother." If that commandment gets high honors, they can leverage it for more financial help and emotional respect from their children.

Over here are a group who raise livestock for a living. To them the top priority commandments are the ones demanding the sacrifice of birds and animals. If Jesus will put his seal of approval on one of THOSE, it will be tremendous for business.

Even the one asking the question—a lawyer—may have an ulterior motive. He knows that one of the commandments has to do with establishing courts of justice. Could this be the most important?

And with 613 laws written in the holy books, no doubt many others in attendance wait anxiously for the answer.

Several factions, each with a different slant on what's essential. Each hoping that Jesus will give their special interest first place when he reveals his take on which commandment is the greatest of all. A delicate situation for sure.

The lawyer who asked the question is quite pleased with himself at this moment, convinced that as soon as Jesus answers, the rabbi will have more foes than friends. There is no way out of this one, he thinks.

But the lawyer is wrong. Jesus answers with some of the strongest words in the Bible. In fact, if we truly believe him, they ARE the strongest words in the Bible.

"'Love the Lord your God with all your heart, with all your soul, and with all your mind.' This is the greatest and most important command. The second is like it: 'Love your neighbor as yourself.'"

Love God and other people, and don't forget to love yourself. This brief quote, taken directly from hundreds of pages of Hebrew scriptures, is—according to Jesus—the most important commandment of them all.

But What If I'm Not Religious?

Not everyone reading this book will be a follower of Christianity or Judaism. They don't have to be. Because nearly every creed has come to the same conclusion that there is nothing more important than loving God and loving our neighbor as we love ourselves.

In fact, it doesn't take any spiritual faith at all to see the importance of loving our neighbor. That truth is built into our very core. It comes out in literature, poetry, art, music, dance— wherever the depths of humanity are expressed.

The dire need for love is all around us. It sounds cliché, even naive, but it's arguable that love could solve nearly all the world's problems. Third world poverty, global hunger, environmental destruction, war—these would all fall before authentic love.

We may not be in a position to impact those issues on a universal scale. We can, however, impact them on a scale as local as the individuals we encounter each day. Poverty, hunger, destruction, broken relationships—these problems exist down the block as well as around the world. And love will go a long way toward overcoming them right where we live.

There are also unseen problems. Personal struggles such as emotional heartache, loneliness, depression, family strife, and the like are epidemic. Loving, one-on-one human interaction may be the ONLY cure for these invisible enemies. People like you and me hold the key.

– – – – – – – – – –

Love God. Love others (our neighbor). Love ourselves. An honest look within tells us nothing is more important.

We've discovered priority one.

6

Who Is My Neighbor?

The story of the Good Samaritan is well known. It's about a person from the town of Samaria who interrupted his commute to help a man who had been robbed, beaten, and left by the side of the road. The Samaritan applied first aid, then took the man to an inn where he could heal. He even paid the bill.

This incident inspired a phrase that's become part of our vernacular. We refer to someone who expresses love in a practical way as a good Samaritan.

What's not so well known is the origin of the Good Samaritan story. It was first told in response to a question posed to a wise teacher. The question was this: "Who is my neighbor?"

"Who is my neighbor?" is a valid thing to ponder, especially in the modern world. Is my neighbor only the person who lives in the house beside mine? Or considering my exposure to news across the globe, should I consider the entire world population as my neighbor?

There's no final word on this, but a few thoughts will suffice.

My neighbor is the person I encounter as I go through normal daily life. He/she is the family next door. And also the barista, cashier, co-worker, friend, and more. Loving my neighbor may involve a brief interaction or a long-term relationship.

"Who is my neighbor?" was the question. And in response came a story which has been preserved for thousands of years. We've heard the answer. Now it's our turn. Someone is lying by the side of the road, in need of help. Let's be good neighbors. Let's be Good Samaritans.

2

Learning To Love

The best portions of a good man's life
are his nameless, unremembered
acts of kindness and love.

– William Wordsworth

In the world of commercial real estate there is a concept known
as "highest and best use." This is the way the value of a property
is determined.

Suppose there's a parcel of land with a gas station on it.
The commercial real estate appraisers don't necessarily consider
the gas station when calculating how much that land is worth.
Instead, they envision the parcel's highest and best use. Perhaps
a gas station really is the best use of that location, but the highest
and best use could be an office building, a college campus, or a
parking lot. The value of the property is based on its highest and
best use, whatever that might be.

Over 2000 years ago, a man claiming to be the son of God
declared that the highest and best use of a human being is to love
God, love his or her neighbor, and love him or her self. Other
religions, people who don't follow any religion, our own hearts,
expressions of humanity, personal observations, the condition
of the world, and events all around us resonate this same truth.
There is nothing more important than love.

It makes sense then that mastering the ability to express
love would be a worthwhile pursuit. And that studying practical

9

ways to show love to others is a good idea.

So let's take a walk down to the local bookstore; even the Christian bookstore. Or perhaps we'll scan books and articles online, look at sermon and lecture topics, check out a few hundred blogs. What will we see?

We will find titles such as *The Ten Steps To This* and *Six Secrets For That.* There are multitudes of self-help manuals and instruction on spiritual topics such as prayer, evangelism, church growth, Bible study, prosperity, faith, fasting, giving, and on and on. Experts claiming to have the keys to material success, physical health, popularity, and more (and who will teach them to us for a fee), seem to be everywhere.

It's as though there is a "how to"—verbal, written, or both—for everything. Well, almost everything.

A void seems to exist for training in one of the highest priorities of all: how, practically, to love another human being, and to love ourselves. Could it be that this supremely important commandment has been lost in the pile of information about every other area of personal development?

Surely authors and teachers aren't oblivious to this topic. The consequences of not loving are apparent every time we hear world news or see how people act on the highway. There must be some other reason for this void.

Maybe the experts think people inherently know how to love. But the evidence says otherwise. Our own experiences, widespread loneliness, self-centeredness—these factors and more point to the fact that people aren't born knowing how to love. So this argument doesn't hold up either.

Perhaps we fear that breaking down the act of loving our neighbor into practical steps diminishes love in some way, reducing it to a sterile, clinical set of techniques that are less than sincere. That would at least be understandable. Unfortunately, though, it leads to a dead end. If we choose to remain in ignorance, how can we increase society's ability to show practical love? Admitting there is a vacuum and doing nothing about it is unacceptable.

Instead, let's take the position that people see the importance of love, that they WANT to love their neighbor and themselves, but they simply don't know how. They realize the necessity, but the skills required to express love in practical ways are rarely (if ever) taught. What's more, those skills do not come naturally, so unpacking them and describing them one by one is not diminishing, it's empowering and vital.

— — — — — — — — — —

Which leads to the motivation for this book. It's an attempt to present ideas for those who want to love in practical ways which others can see and sense. It's a curriculum of sorts, for learning to become an expert in the art of feeling, showing, and acting out of concern for our fellow men and women.

At the same time, it's important to understand the limits of this book.

Love in action could possibly solve even the weightiest problems of mankind, but that is not this book's purpose. These pages are not for healing marriages, solving family grievances, bringing political opponents together, or anything on that scale. Yes, the principles you'll be reading can enhance or even restore relationships of all kinds, but that's not why this was written.

This book is meant to revolutionize people's everyday interactions on the job, in stores, during community events— anywhere humans come in contact with one another. What might begin as casual small talk can become a much deeper connection using the techniques outlined in the chapters to come.

Although the points which follow are in somewhat of a sequence, they are not a step-by-step process. Because love is not a process. Instead, this book offers ideas which form the basis for what is arguably the highest and best use of a human being in relation to other human beings: loving our neighbor as ourselves.

What's Love Got To Do With It?

The English language is interesting. This is especially true of the word "love." English speakers love their spouses. They also love their fishing rods, the New York Yankees, and pepperoni pizza. They love their golden retriever, sunsets, the grandkids, and mystery novels.

Poets romanticize love. Theologians quantify love. Hollywood sensualizes love. Philosophers dissect love.

So when we talk of love, of loving our neighbor, what must that mean? Love for a fishing rod? What's that got to do with it? No wonder we're confused!

Since I'm not a poet, theologian, Hollywood producer, or philosopher, I'll leave those discussions alone. Instead, I'll focus on what the word "love" signifies as it's used in this book.

Love is seeing people as individuals who each have a unique story. Love is truly listening to those people, and asking questions to learn more. It's noticing their needs, taking action, and speaking the truth. Love makes allowances. It also sets boundaries. And let's not forget that love includes loving ourselves.

There are many ways to look at love. Some can't be described. But for showing love in a practical sense, the list above, which we are about to break down and explore, provides a good starting point.

Thanks to Tina Turner, for the use of her song title, "What's Love Got To Do With It." And I know ... not everyone loves the New York Yankees.

PART TWO

The Instruction:
Loving Your Neighbor

3

Love Sees People As Individuals

Jeremiah, the son of Hilkiah,
one of the priests living in Anathoth,
in the territory of Benjamin.

– Jeremiah the Prophet

The surf was cold that night in December 1992 as Luis waded into the Florida Straits, a 93-mile wide strip of saltwater connecting the Gulf of Mexico and the Atlantic Ocean. It's also what separates Cuba, where Luis' life was both miserable and in danger, from the United States.

Around his waist was a rope, tied to a tube that had come from a truck tire. This, propelled by makeshift oars, would— Luis hoped—provide transportation to freedom. He had stolen the tube from the construction yard where he worked sixty hours a week, earning just enough to feed his wife and children, and pay the rent on their one-room home.

Not one to show emotion, Luis resisted tears as he realized he was leaving his family. He dreamt of being able to send for them one day. That was the plan, assuming the *Fuerzas Armadas Revolucionarias*, the Cuban Revolutionary Armed Forces, didn't capture and imprison him. At the moment, he was more worried about sharks.

Time passes, until one day on a humid Tuesday morning, I park my car in the space that says "Reserved For Suite 202" outside the building where my office is located. A short man who appears to be in his early 60s is sweeping trash and depositing it in a dumpster. He's wearing blue jeans and a white t-shirt, which is how I see him every day.

The man catches my eye as I walk toward the employee entrance. He smiles broadly, showing teeth surrounded by a face tanned dark by the Florida sun. "*Hola. Que pasa?*" he asks. "*Nada,*" I reply, using a large portion of my total Spanish vocabulary.

He laughs and goes back to his task. I continue down the hall to the elevator. "It's hard to believe that our maintenance man, Luis, escaped Cuba on a tire tube," I think to myself, and make my morning cup of tea.

— — — — — — — — — —

Everybody Has A Story

As of July 2020, the estimated world population[1] was close to 7.8 billion. That's a big number. What is amazing is that every one of those people has a unique story. Realizing this is the first critical step in learning to love your neighbor.

Not everybody's life has been as dramatic as Luis'. But everyone has a story as unique as a fingerprint or DNA. Where we were born. The family in which we grew up. Brothers and sisters, or no siblings at all. Socio-economic, racial, and other demographic factors. These, plus the nearly infinite mosaic of our experiences, have all brought us to where we are today. This is true of every person we see. It's essential to grasp that in order to truly love our neighbor.

The book of Jeremiah in the Bible begins with an introduction of the author. It says that he is "Jeremiah, the son of Hilkiah, one of the priests living in Anathoth in the territory of Benjamin." He's not just someone who happens to be named Jeremiah. He's not simply a random prophet with a nondescript identity. He is an individual. The son of a certain person who had a certain occupation, and who now resides in a certain place. He has a past. He has a story.

This is true for each person in that world population estimate, including those with whom we come in contact all the time.

The young girl who hands customers their coffee each morning. She is an individual with a story. She is part of a family, complete with unique dynamics. She has a past that includes joyful memories, and possibly a few regrets. She has aspirations for the future, which could be exciting or scaring her right now—perhaps both. And more.

She's not just "the girl at the coffee shop." She's something like this: Gisella, a 21 year-old Latin-American female, daughter of Carlos and Jean, from Pembroke Pines, Florida, who works a summer job as a barista, helps take care of her sick grandmother, struggles with depression since her brother died at age five of childhood leukemia, and will be returning to Southeastern College in six weeks as a senior on a full scholarship. She hopes to continue her education toward a career as a Veterinary Cardiologist, and feels some anxiety about this as her research tells her it's quite difficult to get into vet school. And that is just the beginning. It's only a small percentage of Gisella's story.

The gray-haired man reading nutritional labels in the grocery store. Could he have waded through a rice paddy in Vietnam carrying an M-16 in the 1960s? Perhaps he served as CEO of a company, responsible for scores of employees and millions in revenue. Was he married for several decades to his high school sweetheart, raising a family with her, or did he experience one or more painful divorces?

He's not simply "the old guy at the grocery store." He's so much more.

In our society, people often identify with their occupation. "I'm Lauren. I'm an ER nurse," we say. While this reveals a few things about the type of person Lauren might be and the life she may be living, it's a small piece of the puzzle that makes up a total human being.

Fascinating stories are all around us, locked within people we encounter every day. There are mysteries, dramas, joys and stuggles embodied in each connection. There is so much more to everyone we meet than what we find on the surface. We realize this as we see people as individuals, and only by seeing people as individuals can we begin to love them.

Once Upon A Time ...

If you enjoy hearing a good story, you're in luck, because captivating tales are everywhere.

Benjamin Disraeli (1804-1881), former British Prime Minister said, "Talk to a man about himself, and he will listen for hours." (This likely applies to women also.) True, it doesn't take much to draw stories out of people. That's because people enjoy telling their stories. In fact, they WANT to tell their stories.

Within each of us is the desire to be known, to be seen as an individual with a unique story. Understanding that and providing the opportunity to another person is to bestow a valuable gift. When you give someone the feeling that you see him or her as an individual, and allow that person to share his or her story, you are meeting a profound human need. It's an expression of love.

20

Simply asking "Where are you from?" or "How do you spend your free time?" or "Do you have children?" will often get the ball rolling. After that, some follow up questions combined with sincere interest will usually open the floodgates. Before long, you will be entrenched in a world you could barely imagine: the story of an individual.

It's easy to show sincere interest in people, because people are sincerely interesting. Hearing how Luis risked capture, imprisonment, and life-threatening challenges to cover nearly 100 miles of ocean in a tire tube could keep us on the edge of our seats. What other remarkable experiences have been had by people we encounter every day?

When we see people as individuals and delve into their stories, which they are often glad to tell us, we find that everyone's life is compelling in its own way.

Do you like tales of romance? How about the inside scoop on how fortunes were made and lost? Maybe you go for adventures such as wild journeys or daring explorations. The intricacies of other cultures, details of faraway places, descriptions of life in past decades. Dramas of overcoming poverty, diseases battled, true crime, business deals, daring risks, encounters with the rich and famous—you name it. Every one of these could be as near as the people you see every day.

A subscription to a movie channel isn't required for a front row seat and behind the scenes secrets that are sure to hold our attention. We just need to see people as individuals and let them tell their stories.

So become a bit curious. Invest a little time. Then stand back and be amazed, because you are about to hear some incredible stuff.

A Mindset Shift — Transactional To Relational

Seeing people as individuals requires shifting from a transactional focus to a relational focus. There's a huge difference, and understanding it is essential to practical love. The transactional mindset sees only what's on the surface. Personal encounters are viewed as items to be crossed off a checklist. In this paradigm, the goal is to spend the least amount of time on the task at hand. Take charge, get to the point, finish the encounter, then move on.

Being relational, on the other hand, slows things down and dives deeper. The relational mindset is not in a hurry. It isn't afraid to take a detour or side road if necessary. It pays attention to what's happening around the supposed main topic, knowing that those ancillary issues are sometimes the more significant ones. The relational mindset pauses, takes a breath, asks if there's anything else going on. It lets the other person drive the interaction. It stays engaged.

When a cashier is viewed as someone who hands us a bag as we hand over money, that's transactional. If instead, we see him or her as a living, complex human being with a unique story, not just as a cashier, that's relational.

To the transactional mindset, the barber or hair stylist is there to perform a service while we daydream or stare at our smartphones. The relational mindset knows better, and sees these people as multi-faceted individuals with stories uniquely their own.

This became especially clear to me during a trip to Las Vegas. I found that the cab driver was a ventriloquist, the front desk clerk at the hotel a magician, the bell hop a juggler, and my server at dinner a comedian. Each of them were playing small venues on the side, hoping to be discovered and make it in one of the entertainment hot spots of the world. They had left homes, families, educational opportunities, and careers to chase their dreams. What amazing stories they had, just waiting for the relational mindset to draw them out.

Over time, as the relational mindset takes hold, it affects how we view everyone: those cab drivers, and other fame-seekers in Las Vegas, as well as our co-workers, friends, family, and spouses back home. (Perhaps especially spouses! It's far too easy to slip into a transactional mindset with people we see every day.)

And don't forget the higher end of the economic spectrum. Doctors, attorneys, entrepreneurs, those we consider wealthy, even celebrities and athletes; they have stories as well.

The environment may not always allow us to be one hundred percent relational. We can't explore entire life histories while the checkout line at the grocery store backs up. But we can recognize that those stories exist, and are only uncovered through a relational, rather than transactional, mindset. This shift will also prepare us for additional steps in the art of loving our neighbor.

Approaching someone in a relational manner even briefly can have positive effects. People sense when they are being seen as individuals, rather than being treated as only a means to an end. They light up when they feel that someone cares about their story, regardless of whether or not the situation allows them to tell it.

The next time you're in a restaurant and the server says, "I'm Ben. I'll be taking care of you tonight," try replying, "Hi Ben. What's your day been like?" You might get a look of surprise. Ben is quite aware that he's viewed in a transactional way. He's the guy taking the order, bringing the water, checking to see if everything is okay, and not doing any of this quickly enough for some. You, on the other hand, made a relational connection.

You saw him as an individual—a fellow human being, complete with a unique story—and no doubt that felt good to him. When a lengthy conversation isn't appropriate, it is sometimes possible to extract at least a sliver of the story. This often starts as small talk but can go deep quickly with a slight probe, and lead to future opportunities to engage. This is especially true if the person is dealing with some challenge or difficulty, which just about everyone is at any given time. (We'll dive more into that later.) You might find yourself making plans to meet when you can hear more.

The key point for now is that there are two distinct mindsets for how we view people: transactional and relational. Let's examine our approach and train ourselves to see people in a relational way, as individuals with their own stories.

What's In A Name?

Back in 1936, a traveling salesman named Dale Carnegie wrote a book entitled *How To Win Friends And Influence People.* As of the year 2011 it had sold over 15 million copies, making it one of the best sellers of all time, and had earned the number 19 spot on *Time* magazine's list of the 100 most influential books.

Among the many bits of wisdom Carnegie shared is a reminder that people love to hear the sound of their own names.

People want to be seen as individuals, and a supremely individual aspect of everyone is his or her name. When speaking with people, therefore, a very simple act of showing practical love is to use the person's name.

A challenge we all face is remembering the names of those we just met. There are techniques and gimmicks, and if those work for you, great. But if you prefer not to go that route, just admit you forgot and say, "I'm sorry. I don't remember your name. Would you mind telling me again?" People will be glad to oblige. You don't have to sound like a snake oil peddler with greetings like, "Hi Doug. How are you, Doug? Doug, it's nice to see you. Nice day, Doug, don't you agree?" Mentioning Doug's name every now and then during normal conversation will do. And it will make a big difference in helping him feel loved.

Even THAT Person

Seeing people as individuals applies equally to those we find hard to love, the ones who treat us poorly, and even our enemies. We may not understand why they do what they do. But a sincere attempt to see them as individuals, to get to know their stories, and to interact with them relationally, could bring us closer.

Breaking into a bakery and stealing a loaf of bread is certainly a crime. Although five years in prison seems like an unreasonably harsh punishment, there have to be consequences. And if the perpetrator tries to escape incarceration, an additional penalty could be considered appropriate. But what if the thief was a man desperate to provide food for his unwed sister's starving baby during a time of severe famine in France? Would that affect our sense of what seems fair? This is the dilemma faced by everyone who contemplates the life of Jean Valjean in the novel *Les Misérables*, by Victor Hugo.

That grumpy elderly man who acts impatiently toward the store clerk may have recently lost his wife, just before their 48th anniversary. After a long career focused on making money, he might not be close to his adult children. He has regrets and wonders if his life has counted for anything. If we saw him as an individual and knew his story, we might find it easier to overlook some of the rough edges. Even acknowledging that a story like that is remotely possible should be enough for us to give the man some slack. He's an individual, after all, with a story of SOME sort. Maybe that's all we need to know.

Basic everyday mistakes and worse are often met with a bit more compassion when we know the parties involved. They're not "low-lifes," "idiots," or mere criminals. They're our sons and daughters, brothers and sisters, mothers and fathers, spouses or friends. We may disapprove of their behavior—it might even make us angry—but if we see them as individuals, and know the stories surrounding their actions, we can love them just the same. Shouldn't this also apply to those we may not know as well?

It's easy to bash someone who's been labeled with a term we don't like and to then write him or her off because of it. To say "That person's a liberal" or "a conservative" or "lazy" or "selfish" is far too simple. The truth is that the person is an individual with a huge complex set of factors behind his or her beliefs and actions.

Love demands that we acknowledge all this, see the person—even THAT person—as an individual, open ourselves to his or her story, and approach with a relational mindset.

— — — — — — — — — —

Chapter Summary

Love sees people as individuals. It looks beyond the superficial to recognize that those hotel staff members, men and women in the grocery store, co-workers, neighbors, people in cars on the highway—everyone we meet—are much more than nameless, featureless objects sharing our space.

Human beings are complex; unique combinations of nearly infinite factors. They each have a life story that is probably more amazing and dramatic than we could ever imagine.

People crave to be seen as the individuals they are. To feel that someone is interested in them and their stories in a relational, rather than transactional, way. And to hear the sweetest sound in any language: their names. Fulfilling these desires, even briefly, is a significant way to show love.

Seeing people as individuals with complex stories makes it easier to love those who are different from ourselves, or who hold opinions other than our own. There's much more going on than what we comprehend at first. Stereotypes and quick conclusions no longer work when we look beneath the surface.

As we learn to love our neighbor, the first realization is this: love sees people as individuals.

Beyond Reasonable Doubt

The idea that love sees people as individuals was reinforced when I served on a jury. It was a criminal case, and the two sides were clear as to their missions. The prosecution wanted to convince us that the person whose fate we would decide was guilty beyond a reasonable doubt, and the defense was intent on proving the opposite.

When the prosecuting attorney referred to the gentleman on trial, she used terms such as "the accused" and "the defendant." She stuck to facts and figures when presenting her case.

The defense attorney, on the other hand, asked the young man to stand and face the jury. "This is J_____ S_____," he said. He then repeated his client's name every chance he could. He went into detail about the events of the night in question and what took place before and after the alleged crime.

Clearly, the prosecution's goal was that we, the jury, would not develop any type of personal connection with J_____ S_____. If he could remain only a static object, accused of an illegal act, the fact of his humanity would not affect our decision.

Just as clearly, the defense lawyer wanted us to see his client as a living, breathing person. A human being with a name and a face, and more importantly, with a story.

Each side understood that love sees people as individuals. No doubt about it.

4

Love Listens And Asks Questions

When we are listened to,
it creates us, makes us unfold and expand.

– Brenda Euland

Two frequent travelers sit waiting at the gate in an airport. Looking up from their laptop computers, their eyes meet. A dialogue begins that goes something like this:

Traveler One: "*I sure hope we don't get delayed. I was supposed to be on an earlier flight. Missed my connection due to a mechanical problem out of O'Hare.*"

Traveler Two: "*That happened to me last week leaving LAX. I wound up having to sit in a middle seat on a red eye to make a meeting with my boss the next morning in Baltimore.*"

One: "*I avoid red eyes. I'm Hilton Honors Diamond, so I would have stayed overnight in Los Angeles and told my assistant to set up a WebEx for the meeting.*"

Two: "*I'm a Marriott guy. Their executive lounges are way better than the ones at Hiltons.*"

They will go on like this as long as they have time. Each person talking about himself, while oblivious to what the other is saying.

Someone even coined a humorous term for these interactions: Conversation Poker. The round begins, as it did above, by one person sharing a bit of info, then continues when the next person tops it.

"My grandson just got accepted into Harvard."
"I'll see your grandson at Harvard and raise you my daughter who earned her PhD from Cambridge at age 17."

What's even sadder is that the parties might walk away thinking they had a real conversation. But we know better. Love listens. And love asks questions.

— — — — — — — — —

We previously talked about seeing people as individuals, understanding that everyone has a story, developing a relational rather than transactional mindset, and applying those principles to everyone, whether they agree with us or not. Now we're on to the next step: listen. Listen to find out what that person's story is. And ask questions to learn more.

True listening is uncommon. And that goes for scenarios far beyond casual encounters at airports. The family dinner table conversation has become rare to non-existent, thanks to busy lives, demanding careers, and technology that separates as much as it connects. Co-workers don't share lunches or happy hours like they used to, and when it does happen, there's far more talking than listening.

Ironically, listening to others and asking questions may be the easiest part of learning how to love. That's because people are so eager to tell their stories. A wise listener who also knows how to make caring inquiries will have no shortage of opportunities.

— — — — — — — — —

Let's revisit the dialogue between the two frequent travelers in the airport from the beginning of this chapter. It begins just as it did before, but imagine it progressing differently.

Traveler One: "*I sure hope we don't get delayed. I was supposed to be on an earlier flight. Missed my connection due to a mechanical problem out of O'Hare.*"

Traveler Two: "*Oh no. I'm sorry to hear that. Where are you headed?*"

One: "*Phoenix.*"

Two: "*Ahh. What's in Phoenix?*"

One: "*My mom. She had a stroke. Not sure what I'm walking into, but I need to get there ASAP.*"

Two: "*That must be a lot for you to bear. How are you holding up?*"

From here, Traveler Two will be able to continue taking steps toward showing true compassion. There's no telling where things could lead, but this conversation is certainly unlike the first one that started the same way.

– – – – – – – – –

People will almost always talk if someone will listen. And not just about their struggles. They are equally enthusiastic about sharing good news regarding themselves, their families, and friends. They want to discuss books they have read, hobbies, accomplishments, education, careers, and more. Remember, everybody has a story, and virtually every man and woman alive loves talking about it.

So how do we listen in a way that makes people feel loved? Let's explore.

– – – – – – – – –

Hearing People Into Existence

Laurie Buchanan, PhD said, "When we listen, we hear someone into existence." What a profound statement. People are caught in confusing and difficult circumstances. They have problems. They feel challenged. They also have situations that make them happy. In the midst of this, they are struggling on the job, trying to carve out an existence that counts for something, and are pulled in many directions. It's not easy to figure themselves out.

One way to unravel the gnarled, twisted, tangled elements of life is to write or talk about them. That's why journaling is so beneficial. Sometimes, though, it's better to have a caring human being available and willing to engage in conversation. But finding one who will listen is rare—extremely rare.

That's where Dr. Laurie Buchanan's beautiful quote applies. As people talk and we listen, asking questions along the way, we help them organize their thoughts. Things become clearer to them as they discover new ways of looking at their situations. They find ideas they have never considered before. We are hearing those people into existence. It's a valuable contribution to make to a person's life.

Give The Other Person Your Full Attention

We live in a world of distractions so numerous that listing even a fraction of them would be impossible. There are externals such as all the magical apps on our phones that scream to be tapped, swiped, clicked, read, and responded to. Just as real are the internal distractions, those inside our minds. Thoughts as diverse as planning for retirement and replenishing the cat litter box pop into our heads without warning, demanding to be noticed ... right now! Although it has not become an official psychological diagnosis as of the writing of this book, there is a term for that dilemma. It's called "urgency addiction."

Urgency addiction is a major topic among business publications and consultants. When we accomplish any success, no matter how small, such as deleting an email or responding to a text message if only to say "Thanks," our brains release a shot of dopamine. This chemical is connected to feelings of pleasure and motivation. It's the same effect that occurs under the influence of opioids (at a much smaller dosage of course). We want to repeat the action that caused the pleasant sensation, so we look again to see if there is anything new in our inbox or social media feed. We can even experience a sense of withdrawal if we go very long without giving in to the urge. It's a serious problem affecting people's productivity, as well as their ability to show love.

Concentrating on anything for more than a few seconds is rare. But that is precisely what is required in order to listen to others in a way which expresses love. We have got to ignore both our external and internal clutter in order to give something our full attention.

Simply becoming aware when we're beginning to chase distractions is a step in the right direction. If we catch ourselves drifting away from the conversation, we have a better chance of bringing ourselves back.

Tactics as basic as turning off the TV, exiting the email program, or putting the phone on airplane mode can be highly effective. It's a small price to pay for learning to love.

Always have a notepad and pen ready. You can't stop distracting thoughts such as, "Buy more cat litter," from entering your mind. By capturing them in writing, however, you can overcome their power to compete with the precious person in front of you or on the phone sharing his or her story. Later, you will go back to your list and deal with whatever is on it.

Many people think the ability to multi-task is admirable. But doing more than one thing at a time is humanly impossible. People do not multi-task. Instead, they're switching their focus back and forth between more than one stimulus. A more accurate term is "focus-shifting." This is not compatible with effective listening.

We cannot truly listen to another person while watching the game or the stock ticker. Focus-shifting might not be a problem during casual conversation, where missing a few points is no big deal, but it won't do for creating connections.

As basic as it sounds, looking someone in the eye will help you maintain your attention and project a caring attitude. Letting your gaze wander around the room has the opposite effect; the person will conclude that you're not interested. (Of course don't stare into the other person's eyes the whole time you're together. That would be creepy.)

If you find it awkward to look at someone's pupils, train yourself to focus on the bridge of their nose. They will never know the difference.

And you have heard this before, but it's worth repeating: Don't use the time while the other person is speaking to think about what you are about to say. If you need a minute to get your thoughts together, simply let him or her know that while you ponder in silence.

So do whatever it takes to tune out distractions, stop trying to multi-task, look the person in the eye, and resist the urge to compose your reply while he or she is speaking. You will be on your way to giving another human being your full attention. And this type of listening expresses love in a practical way.

Ask Questions

Remember the two conversations between the travelers in the airport earlier in this chapter? A few questions were the difference between a self-centered interaction and one that made a connection. An important element for effective listening, therefore, is this: ask questions.

Everyone has concerns, emotional pain, worries, and the like. Despite longing for someone who will listen, they are often not willing to reveal those parts of themselves all at once. Even people who are talkative and seem to be transparent are usually hiding something deeper. Before opening up, they want to know that the person who will be hearing what they have to say truly cares.

Appropriate questions bridge the gap. They show that we really are interested. They draw people out. At the same time, we don't want to appear meddlesome, or make people feel they're being interrogated. It's important to know when to back off. There is no perfect rule for this, but a good guideline might be to ask three questions based on your listening, then reevaluate.

Here's another example, using a conversation that happens every Monday morning in hundreds of offices. We'll call these people Terry and Gene.

Terry: *"What did you do this weekend?"*
Gene: *"I took my family to a movie."*
Terry: *"Oh, that's interesting. I took my family to a movie too. I can't believe how overpriced movies are these days. And the popcorn, my goodness, seven dollars for a box. It's ridiculous. Well, back to work. Good talking to you."*

Terry failed to ask a question, and the result was a lack of anything meaningful at all. Using the three-question technique, the conversation might go like this:

Terry: "*What did you do this weekend?*"
Gene: "*I took my family to a movie.*"
Terry: "*Oh, that's interesting. What movie?*"
Gene: "*The new adventure film that's out.*"
Terry: "*How did you like it?*"
Gene: "*Personally I thought it was well done, but it might have been too intense for the kids.*"
Terry: "*Yeah, I can understand. I happened to see the same movie this weekend myself. You're right; there were some pretty scary scenes.*"

Terry might follow up now or later, talking about Gene's family, the challenges of parenting, or the effect of movies on children. It's remarkable how quickly a conversation can go from small talk to something much more with just three questions.

It doesn't always happen that the conversation goes deeper, and that's okay. Not every interaction has to be profound. So if the dialogue remains shallow, this may not be the time to dig. Just go with it and enjoy.

What If I'm Shy?

People who consider themselves shy may think that asking questions will be a difficult part of loving their neighbor. That's a valid fear. Let's look into it.

There are those who feel near terror just thinking about interacting with a casual acquaintance or stranger. But another human trait is in the shy person's favor; people are eager to tell their stories, and they will do so with just the slightest nudge. Once they feel someone cares, and the ball gets rolling, you won't have to say much.

So whether or not you have the courage to ask questions,

you can become a master listener. With the slightest indication that you are opening the door via a phrase like, "How interesting," "No kidding?" or simply, "Wow!"—or even non-verbal cues such as an inquisitive facial expression—people will usually share their stories freely.

Not comfortable talking about yourself? That is seldom a concern. People will be so engaged in telling their own stories that they will barely notice. This is not a criticism. They're sorely in need of love, and by being a willing listener, you are providing that.

**Listen For The Feeling ... Find The Feeling ...
Connect With The Feeling**

People's narratives have many layers. On the surface are basic data points: names, dates, places. A conversation may start there, but that is rarely what individuals actually want to discuss. At a much deeper level are the feelings which come with the story. Loving our neighbor involves going beneath the mere facts in order to listen for, find, and connect with those feelings.

Here's an absurd (hopefully) example. A father and his adult son leave a restaurant. As they get near the son's car, they notice a fresh scrape where the door was obviously sideswiped while they were eating.

The son runs over to his car, raises both arms in the air and shouts, "[Expletive], look what somebody did to my car! The door is totally smashed."

His dad replies, "It's true, Son, that another vehicle made contact with your car. But I wouldn't call that smashed. More like scraped. And did you know that a staggering fourteen percent of all auto insurance claims are due to parking lot incidents?"

While the dad did listen to the words his son said, he only heard that there was damage to the car. The feelings were completely missed.

A more loving approach would have been to listen for, find, and connect with the feeling rather than only addressing the details. This would have prompted a reply from the father such as, "Oh no! How terrible. That really stinks."

From there, the conversation could go in many directions, but it's off to a good and loving start, largely because Dad connected with his son's feelings.

You may have noticed that the son's feelings were largely expressed non-verbally. He ran to the car, put both hands in the air, and shouted when he spoke. Physical actions and tones of voice reveal the emotions beneath the words. They can point to anything from disappointment to elation. Keep an eye and ear open for them.

Many people are not aware of the full range of their emotions. They only know that they either feel good or they feel bad, and not much beyond that. To love others in practical ways will require expanding our sensitivity to a broader spectrum of feelings, then building our vocabulary of words that differentiate each of those feelings. If we are speaking with someone who cannot identify how he or she feels, we may be able to help.

According to psychologists, there are seven basic emotions: anger, contempt, disgust, fear, happiness, sadness, and surprise. What's more, research has concluded that these are universal across all of mankind, regardless of culture, geographic location, or any other factor. People in New Guinea, New Mexico, and New England all feel the same seven. So anyone who happens to be human has the capacity for a more comprehensive scope of emotions than merely "bad" or "good."

Still, those of us who aren't well versed in such areas may

find it difficult to describe what someone is feeling (or even what we ourselves are feeling), using only seven words. So here is a longer list:

—Words associated with positive feelings: amazed, appreciative, bold, brave, calm, cheerful, contented, delighted, excited, festive, free, great, happy, joyful, jubilant, optimistic, proud, respectful, serene, strong, upbeat, wonderful

—Words associated with negative feelings: aggravated, angry, awful, cold, concerned, depressed, disappointed, dreary, grumpy, mad, miserable, moody, nervous, pessimistic, sad, sour, tearful, terrible, tired, weak

Remembering a few of these words, and learning when they apply, will make a huge difference as we attempt to form bonds with others. We will be able to connect with people who feel aggravated, depressed, or nervous, rather than only "bad." Or with those feeling bold, excited, or upbeat, rather than just "good."

At times it's helpful if you voice what the other person might be feeling. In the scenario involving the sideswiped car, this could mean the father saying, "You must be very angry right now" or "How could anyone do that without even leaving a note? That's aggravating." We want to be careful with this, however, because people are sometimes offended when others make assumptions about what's on their minds.

We may not always know what the person is feeling. A job transfer to another city could be good news or bad news. If we reply, "Wow! I'm so happy for you," when he or she is concerned about uprooting the kids from the local drama club, we have not only failed to connect with the feeling, we might even seem insensitive. A simple work around is to ask, "How do you feel about that?" when you are not sure. Once you have an answer, the path to a meaningful connection will be clear.

If a person gives a response such as, "Okay I guess," you will have an opportunity to use your glossary of emotion words. You might reply, "Are you excited about the new job or kind of concerned?" This will help the person define what he or she is going through and be better able to deal with it. The rest of the discussion can follow suit.

When we ask questions, then listen for, find, and connect with the feeling, we give the other person space to share more. The conversation can continue until it logically plays out.

You Did WHAT?! vs. I Can Handle It

It's critical to keep a handle on your reactions to whatever you're told, no matter how fantastic, sad, or even shocking. The stories we hear will include every level of boasting and confession. We've got to show that we can handle anything.

A gasp when someone tells you of a grave mistake from the past will undoubtedly shut down future bonding. On the other hand, a blank stare when your friend just got engaged, or a beloved pet died, will give the impression that you are not at all interested.

The person who closed a business deal and made a million dollars profit needs to know that you're happy for his or her good fortune. "That's tremendous," you might say. "Let's go out and celebrate." (Hopefully your friend will pick up the tab.)

If someone admits to an extramarital affair, exclaiming, "You did WHAT?!" would be the wrong response. Instead, something like, "That's a serious matter. How did it affect you and your family?" stated with the right body language and tone of voice, will make a genuine connection and keep the story rolling.

Avoid making judgments. We live in a judgmental society, where people are constantly criticized and often feel condemned. A listening ear from a person who doesn't flinch or give any indication of abandoning the relationship no matter what skeletons come to the surface is supremely appreciated. On the flip side, stating what you think the person "should" have done, comparing him or her unfavorably to someone else, expressing personal displeasure or disappointment in the person, and similar judgments will likely cause the person to hide his or her real self in the future. (We'll unpack this more in a future chapter.)

This does not mean we approve of every behavior. If the person intentionally acted in some negative way, we call it what it is. But we speak only to the behavior and not to the overall character of the person. An extramarital affair is a grievous matter. It does not, however, give us the right to define the total identity and character of the person. Humans are far too complex for that. (There may be a point where we can speak to someone's overall identity and character, but that requires a much deeper level of relationship than we're discussing in this book.)

The "I can handle it" response dovetails with listening for, finding, and connecting with the feeling. People have to know we have heard their stories, we get their feelings, and everything they told us has landed in a safe place.

Share Yourself, But Don't Overdo It

We make people feel loved by giving them our full attention, asking questions, listening for, finding, and connecting with the feeling, and letting them know we can handle whatever they have to say. But communication is a two-way street. Even the neediest individuals want to honor that, plus they may enjoy hearing our stories as well.

When one person is doing all the sharing, eventually he or she can feel like a project, a case, or a patient in therapy, rather than a friend or peer. The way to keep the relationship healthier is to share a little about yourself. (There is nothing wrong with being in therapy, but that's not the focus of this book.)

We do, however, have to make sure we're not oversharing. Pay attention to the number of times you use the word "I". If you hear "I" in the sound of your own voice too frequently, you might have crossed the line.

For example, when speaking to someone who has been downsized out of a job, it's okay to say, "I remember getting laid off once. It was hard to go home that day, because I was too depressed to tell my family." If a person's story includes the loss of a loved one, perhaps you would say, "My mother passed away eight years ago. I still miss her terribly every day." To a friend enjoying the purchase of a new car, maybe, "Bringing home my first new car was one of the most exciting days of my life." (Notice that in each of these cases, we have used language that connects with a feeling.) Getting into the details of your story, however, is not advisable unless the other person indicates a clear desire to hear more.

Be careful not to hijack the conversation—that is, to turn the conversation around and make it about you. Your story may be interesting, but it does not have greater importance than the other person's.

Sharing about yourself can show you are willing to be vulnerable. It creates a larger, more secure place for someone to open up. After you have revealed a little of your own story, wait to see how the other person reacts. If he or she asks to know more, carry on. If not, that is your cue to ask a question about the other person's life and pick up the conversation there.

And although there are few absolute rules for effective listening, here is one to remember: It's best not to say "I know how you feel."

There is no way that any person can truly know how another person feels. Humans are far too complicated. "I know how you feel" diminishes the other person's emotions, builds a barrier between people, and can even cause resentment. It almost always creates a roadblock to further connection.

The key to effectively sharing yourself is this: do it, but don't overdo it.

I Relate ... Mostly

People who want to help others often think that talking about themselves will show how well they relate to what the other person is saying, creating a strong connection. There could be some truth to that, but only in specific situations.

An amusing short story called "Makes The Whole World Kin," published in 1911 by the writer O. Henry, addresses this. It's the tale of a man who wakes up in the middle of the night to find a burglar in his bedroom. The burglar points a gun and demands that the man put his hands in the air. But the one getting robbed is unable to lift one of his arms and explains why; he has rheumatism in the shoulder.

Coincidentally, the burglar has the same rheumatoid ailment. The two begin to discuss remedies for reducing inflammation and pain. Here's an excerpt from the conversation:

"Ever try rattlesnake oil?"
"Gallons," responds the burglar.
"Some use Chiselum's Pills."

"Fudge!" said the burglar. "Took 'em five months. No good."

As they banter over their mutual affliction, a bond is formed. Eventually the burglar puts his gun away and invites the homeowner out for drinks, even offering to pay the bill.

Sharing about ourselves won't necessarily have an outcome like the O. Henry story. At first it might seem to make sense that we would feel closer to a person who has gone through something similar to our own experience. But that is not always the case because people's lives are unique, and no one has faced exactly what someone else has in all its complexity. With the broad strokes of our own experience we can sometimes create a link that is beneficial, but it's best not to put too much emphasis on your own story while someone else is telling theirs.

Keep Confidences

When people tell you their stories, you're going to hear everything from the hilarious to the horrible. Some of it will have high potential as interesting tidbits you could whisper to friends, family, or in the office lunchroom. Avoid that temptation at all costs. Talking about people behind their backs will erode your value as a listener and your reputation as someone who expresses love.

Failing to keep confidences causes lost credibility in several ways. The person you betrayed will likely never confide in you again. And when you remark to someone that, "April told me this, but don't repeat it," you send a message that you can't be trusted. Now that person will think twice before opening up about anything sensitive.

You may think that telling someone's tale of overcoming an adversity may help another person. While that could be true, it's not advisable unless you have specific permission to do so. Don't even take a chance by relaying a situation and solution without revealing a name or details. People are good at filling in the blanks and deciphering what you thought was a hidden identity. Being on the listening end of people's stories is a privilege. We must not violate that. The consequences of being labeled as someone who cannot be trusted are severe. It is simply imperative to keep confidences.

(Note: Counseling professionals are required to report anyone who is suicidal, homicidal, or abusing a child or elderly person. While those situations are outside the scope of this book, should you encounter such an individual, do contact someone who can help.)

Open-Door Policy

There are times when people want to talk with someone right then. It's not an outright emergency, but they are facing a challenge, good fortune has smiled and they would like to share the news, or they're confused and looking for a brainstorming partner. Unfortunately, they can't think of one person to whom they could reach out in that moment.

That is where you and I come in. By signaling to people that we don't consider it an intrusion when they contact us (with reasonable frequency at reasonable times of the day or evening), we are expressing love in a hugely significant way.

Of course there are limits to our capabilities. We have families which must take priority. We can't speak with more than one person simultaneously or answer the phone at 2:00 a.m. very often while maintaining a full life. Finding this balance will be discussed in Chapter 9.

Many reading this would be glad to listen any time. But problems arise when others are not aware you feel that way. People may be afraid they will wake you during morning hours, interrupt you during the workday, disrupt your dinner in the early evening, or catch you as you're getting ready for bed. Or they may simply think, "He/she is too busy in general."

A good practice that can circumvent this is to make it known that you are happy to hear from people and consider it an honor. Should they catch you at a time that is not convenient, you will let them know and arrange for the next best opportunity.

If you want to love your neighbor in a practical way by being a listener, the open-door policy is an effective way to do it.

Silence Can Be Golden

At its highest level, the act of listening and asking questions is about creating a human connection. Words can do that, but silence also has the power to connect people.

I remember being in the hospital after an accident. My injuries were such that the timetable for healing was uncertain. Each day contained a large question mark, as I waited anxiously for the doctor to tell me if any progress had been made which would take me closer to being discharged. Dozens of people called. Many came to visit. They asked questions and listened as I told my story and shared what I was going through.

One evening a very special friend walked into my room. Without saying a word, she sat in the chair by my bed and just looked me in the eye. It was quite a while before she spoke; a minute or so can seem very long when you're staring at one another's pupils.

Eventually she must have seen what she had been looking

for. "There, I found you," she said. "I knew you were in there." We hugged, and a few moments later, she left. Very few words were exchanged, but it was a profoundly intimate experience. It's great to ask questions and listen. And then there are the times when silence does the job equally as well.

— — — — — — — — —

Chapter Summary

Everyone is an individual with a story. People would generally like to tell that story if only someone would listen. Those of us who endeavor to love our neighbor in practical ways realize this and work at becoming expert listeners, because we know that listening and asking questions can be transformational.

When people talk, they process their thoughts, finding clarity and new ways of looking at situations. But talking requires a listener. As Laurie Buchanan, PhD said, "When we listen, we hear someone into existence."

Listening deserves our full attention. We ask questions, and in the dialogue which follows, we listen for and find the emotions behind the person's words, then provide feedback which demonstrates a connection with those feelings. If we can't identify what the person is feeling, we ask.

By keeping our reactions at an appropriate level, no matter what the person tells us, we create a safe place for that person. He or she gains a sense that we can handle whatever might come up, without judgment or condemnation.

It may sometimes be beneficial to share parts of our own story, as long as we don't overdo it. Aside from adding interest to the conversation, this can strengthen the bond between us and another person. In this way, we show we trust him or her, sending signals that this is a special relationship where there is no need to be afraid to reveal anything. But we are careful not to hijack the conversation by turning it around and making it about ourselves. And we resist the glib statement, "I know how you feel."

We keep what we're told in strict confidence, realizing the honor people have given us by relating their stories. (If someone is suicidal, homicidal, or abusing a child or elderly person, that information must be reported to someone who can help.)

An open-door policy which lets people know we don't consider their reasonable contacts with us as intrusions is an effective practical way to show love.

Despite the power and significance of asking questions and listening, there are times when silence can be even more effective than words for creating a human connection.

These abilities make us the type of listeners with whom people want to talk. And why is that important? Because love listens. And love asks questions.

Do Talk To Strangers

When we were children most of us were told by our parents, "Don't talk to strangers." That was good advice at the time. But we are no longer children, and we want to show love to others. So let's embrace a new mindset and converse with people wherever we are.

The cashier at the grocery store, the valet at the theater, and the man sitting alone at the diner are all examples of people we can see as individuals. They are humans who have stories, so we listen even if only for a moment.

It might begin with a simple, "How are you today?" in a voice that shows you really care about the answer. One or two follow up questions may be all time allows. But even a small deposit invested in another human is significant. And we never know, those people might become close friends over time. Lots of lasting relationships have started this way.

Thanks, Mom and Dad, for watching out for us with a wise warning. It's time now that we watch out for others. One way we are going to do that is by striking up a quick chat here and there. We're going to talk to strangers.

5

Love Notices The Need

We're very needy people, you know.
– Alex Van Halen

On the morning of September 25, 2000, 19-year old Kevin Hines waved goodbye to his father, Pat, as Pat dropped him off at City College in their hometown of San Francisco. Kevin was expected to attend class that day, but he had something else in mind. He promptly boarded a bus for the Golden Gate Bridge where he planned to jump to his death.[1]

Hines suffered from bipolar disorder, manifesting in paranoia, mood swings, voices, and hallucinations. His girlfriend recently broke up with him. Just months ago he'd moved in with his father after a major disagreement with his mother with whom Kevin had lived since his parents divorced a few years earlier. He was constantly depressed. Strangely, however, he felt a little better this morning, believing that the pain would soon be over for good.

Walking along the Golden Gate's pedestrian path, Kevin began to cry. He was confused, even conflicted. Voices in his head urged him to jump. Yet there was a small desire to stay alive.

Kevin made a decision. If just one person would stop and show concern for him, he would abandon the idea of suicide, at least for now. He shuffled along, sobbing visibly, waiting for somebody to ask if he was okay, though he clearly was not.

A security officer, bridge workers, and countless pedestrians passed by. An obviously distraught young man, at the spot where a person has taken his or her own life every two weeks on average since 1937, and yet no one seemed to notice. Perhaps there really was only one way out.

Finally, a woman approached. Looking at Kevin, she spoke. Could this be a sign of hope? With a slight German accent, the woman posed a question to him. She wanted to know if he would take her picture.

Seconds later, Kevin Hines climbed over the rail of the Golden Gate Bridge, 220 feet above San Francisco Bay, and leapt.

— — — — — — — — — —

The story of Kevin Hines has a much happier ending than it could have. Miraculously, he survived, with the help of a sea lion; yes, a sea lion. Today he is active as an advocate for suicide prevention. You can learn more of this amazing story from articles and videos all across the internet, and in his book, *Cracked, Not Broken: Surviving and Thriving After a Suicide Attempt.*

Kevin Hines' experience underscores much of what we have been learning. Here was a complex human being, desperately wanting to be seen as an individual, yet to those around him, he remained nondescript, just another sightseer at a famous landmark. He craved a listening ear. Instead the one person who engaged with him was concerned only with her own agenda.

The people on the Golden Gate Bridge with Kevin that day don't necessarily warrant our anger or disapproval. They reflect the typical condition of humanity. Sadly, we have not been taught the fundamentals of loving our neighbor, and the concepts don't come naturally.

Which leads to our next point: the discipline of noticing the need.

— — — — — — — — —

Social Relations

Some rudimentary internet research, using questions such as, "How many people will I meet in my lifetime?" returned answers ranging from 472 to over 80,000. That is far from conclusive, but it's clear that each of us will have some level of contact with a significant number during our time on Earth.

Social scientists discuss what they call "social relations," meaning any interaction between two or more individuals.

Think of all the social relations each of us encounter in a week or even a day. They occur at the sub shop, the gym, the diner, on the job, in line at any store, at a gas station, a theater, sitting on a park bench, walking on the beach, watching the kids' soccer games, and more.

Whether interacting with one person at a time or a crowd of thousands, the people we engage intentionally or simply stumble upon at random have needs. If we're serious about loving our neighbor, we should try to notice.

The restaurant server taking your order ... does he seem a little down? Has a co-worker been acting strangely? Does the neighbor no longer wave when she walks past your house? Is your child's friend always wearing the same clothes? Has a car in the driveway down the block not moved for weeks?

These behaviors and situations may have reasonable explanations, but they could be signs of real needs. It's important for someone to notice. That's you.

Ninety-Nine To One

A woman who collected antique music boxes had one hundred of them in a display case. Or so she thought. One morning as she was counting, the tally came to ninety-nine.

She could barely believe it. "I dusted these just the other day. I'm sure they were all here."

What does this woman do? She scours her mind for any clue as to how this could have happened. She calls people who might know anything about the situation, thinks of everyone who had access to her collection, contacts pawn shops and antique dealers in case the missing music box shows up. She doesn't say to herself, "I still have ninety-nine music boxes. Why should I care about only one?" No, she leaves the ninety-nine where they are and looks for the one that is lost.

This is the mentality of those who notice people's needs. In a networking event, the cafeteria, or any group gathering, they are looking for the one who appears to be neglected—anybody who seems to be by him or herself, not engaging with the crowd. They are more concerned with the needs of the one than with the masses who have plenty.

Maybe the person who's alone is new to that setting and would welcome an introduction. Perhaps he or she is in the midst of something difficult and feels isolated, longing for human interaction. Of course sometimes people are enjoying the solitude, even in public, so it's wise to be sensitive just in case.

Either way, noticing the one who is not engaging with the ninety-nine, and considering that the person may have a need, is an act of practical love.

Everyone Has A Need

To love our neighbors, it's important to realize that every person
has some sort of need. This is not as obvious as it sounds. People
interact for hours without considering anything beyond the
immediate small talk. They watch sports together on television
or play cards in a group for years, yet never go beneath the
surface in their conversations.

Sure, at times it's appropriate to just chat. Even then, it
is wise to remain mindful that someone may be hiding a need
under the smiles, seemingly positive attitude, or appearance of
success. If nothing resembling a need surfaces, that is perfectly
fine. But if some need does reveal itself, we won't miss it if we are
being consciously perceptive.

Don't be fooled by society's reluctance for people to expose
their needs. "Fine, thanks, and you," is a trained response to,
"How are you?" But surely it doesn't always tell the whole story.

It is quite likely that you could walk up to any person
anywhere; at a restaurant, a shopping center, in line at the grocery
store, on the job, you name it. You could catch that person's
eye—a perfect stranger—and say, "I'm sorry for what you're
going through right now," and in the majority of instances, he or
she would know exactly what you're talking about, even though
you had no idea. Some significant challenge or difficulty is close
to the top of most people's minds all the time.

Not all needs are due to something negative. People have a
need to express their joys as well. So imagine approaching those
same random strangers and saying, "I'm so happy for you. You
must be excited by that recent event." It's a safe bet they will
immediately apply what you said to something specific in their
own lives, a family member's, or friend's.

In either case, these people would be touched because
someone noticed their need. They might never suspect that your

statement was arbitrary. It's universal that everyone has some sort of need.

"Notice" Is A Verb

The crowds were waiting for Jesus and his colleagues as they disembarked from their boat after crossing the Sea Of Galilee. And why not? This young rabbi was gaining a reputation for doing miracles. There was no telling what might happen. The scene was chaotic.

Suddenly, Jesus spoke. "Who touched me?" he asked.

"Who touched you?" one of his friends replied. "People are pressing on you from all sides. What do you mean, 'Who touched me?' Dozens of people are touching you."

But Jesus was in tune to people. He knew someone had touched him in a special, desperate way. Someone with a need.

Sure enough, a woman came forward and admitted it was her. She explained her situation: a medical issue which no doctor had been able to diagnose or treat, despite her spending her life savings seeking help. In the midst of the activity of a crowd, Jesus noticed a need.

To notice the needs of others requires a sort of mental radar scanner running in the back of our minds. And like a radar scanner, which will only work when the power switch is in the "On" position, we have got to be deliberate, actively aware of people all around us no matter where we find ourselves. Noticing needs won't happen automatically.

As children, we were told to "pay attention." Now we can apply that to an important human endeavor: loving our neighbor by noticing the need.

Training The Muscle

There are exercises we can perform which will strengthen our ability to notice the needs of others.

Learning to make general observations is a first step. Whenever you are in a room or car, including where you are right now, you can work to heighten your perception. Start with colors. Look around. What do you see that's green? Got that? Now do it again, picking out anything blue. Red. Yellow.

Look for items that might be out of place. Is a picture on the wall hanging crooked? Is there something nearby that is broken?

Continue the exercise by finding the beauty around you. You might see flowers or artwork. Some common object that's especially well designed may catch your eye.

Now take a big step. Direct your focus at human beings. Next time you are around one or more people, see if you can detect a need. It can be something physical (a person carrying a heavy package), emotional (someone who looks sad), or spiritual (a man or woman who seems to lack purpose in life), because needs come in all these areas.

Sometimes people's words are enough. They state their needs outright. But often you must read between the lines. Facial expressions, body language, and tone of voice reflect people's needs as well. (And remember "Listen For The Feeling" from a previous chapter.)

Engage your sense of hearing in other ways as well. Are there sounds in addition to voices which might signal a need? Also, intuition is often thought of as a sort of sixth sense. Does your intuition prompt you to notice anything that feels like a person's need?

Noticing needs may not come naturally, but these exercises will train us in this critical aspect of showing love.

It's All About The Shoes

There is an old saying in business circles that you can tell a lot about people by looking at their shoes. While it may or may not be true, some eighth-grade students in Bellevue, Nebraska proved they were highly skilled at noticing shoes, and at noticing the need as well.

Early in the year 2020, Trey Payne,[2] a teacher and coach at Logan Fontenelle Middle School, discovered one day that his expensive gray Nike Kevin Durant 12 sneakers were missing, very likely stolen. Mr. Payne asked around if anyone had seen them. With no leads to follow, according to his own words, "After that I let it go completely."

A little over two weeks later, Trey was presented with a gift bag during his fifth period class. A self-proclaimed expert at guessing presents, Trey stated, "I hope this isn't shoes, guys. Oh my. Are you serious?" Then he opened the bag, saw what was inside, and began to cry.

They were shoes, for sure. Mr. Payne's students pooled their money and replaced the teacher's loss. But more significantly, they were the exact same model and color of KD12 shoes as the ones which had disappeared. These teenagers had paid close attention, providing a superb example of noticing the need.[3]

Brain Science And Love

A human brain contains tiny spaces called synapses. Researchers at the Stanford University School of Medicine estimate the number of synapses in a healthy adult brain at "hundreds of trillions."[4] Electrical impulses travel through these spaces all the time. There is no way we can deal with all this activity on a practical basis, so it's good to know that the brain itself has a built-in solution.

Neuroscientists speak of what is called the reticular activating system (RAS). The RAS is a network of neurons in the brain stem which have several functions affecting our behavior. Please don't take that definition to the medical community, as it is nowhere near scientifically comprehensive, though the basic idea is accurate.

What's important to our discussion is that the RAS acts as a filter, blocking certain input from the brain, and letting other stimuli through. This explains why a new mother living in a downtown high rise can sleep through the sounds of the city, including loud horns and sirens, but instantly awakens at the first whimper from the baby's crib. On the other hand, it is why the person driving the ice cream truck doesn't hear the music anymore, even though it plays over and over and over and over …

In a famous research experiment, and the book written as a result, authors Christopher Chabris and Daniel Simons demonstrated this phenomenon beautifully. Their work clearly shows that people easily overlook something obvious when their focus is elsewhere. I'm tempted to describe the experiment, but I don't want to spoil the fun for anyone who hasn't seen it. Do an internet search for "selective attention test" and watch the video.[5] You'll get the point.

The astonishing truth is that we can train our RAS. The process for this is called reticular formation, which was discussed as far back as the May 1957 issue of *Scientific American*[6] Through reticular formation you can aim your RAS in a direction, and it will respond in kind.

Have you noticed that as soon as you start thinking about buying a particular make and model of car, you seem to see those cars everywhere? Or when you learn a new word, you hear it in conversations all around you? That's because you are focusing your reticular activating system on those specifics through reticular formation.

You used reticular formation in a previous section of this book. ("Training The Muscle") When you looked for items of a certain color, your RAS let objects of that color come through, and filtered out anything that was another color.

Imagine that a person we'll call Brendan is watching a movie with someone who had a long career as a Hollywood director of major motion pictures. Brendan enjoys the plot, and may even notice elements of the dialogue, music, acting, and cinematography. But the former director will see nuances and detail that go beyond Brendan's ability to comprehend. When it comes to movies, the director has an RAS which has been formed through years of training.

It's up to each of us to be intentional about what we want brought to our attention. With some reticular formation exercise, people's needs will become more apparent.

Noticing The Need For Privacy

Questions are an effective way to let people know we are listening. Now, as we address noticing people's needs, let's consider an alternate aspect; in certain cases the more loving route is to realize the need to NOT ask questions.

One chilly October morning a few years back started like so many days of my life. But soon, things got interesting. While out for an easy four-mile run, staying on the sidewalk for safety's sake, I was hit by a motorized, gas-powered, heavy, cruiser style bicycle. The impact came from behind, so there was no escape. I guess somehow the rider didn't see me.

The hour or so which followed is a blur of vague memories. Passing out twice. Strapped to a board inside an ambulance with sirens blaring and lights flashing. EMTs shouting at me to keep me awake. My diagnosis was four broken ribs and a collapsed, punctured lung, along with a gash in my head requiring four staples.

During seven days in the hospital, and for weeks thereafter, I received more phone calls, emails, text messages, and social media direct messages than I could count. They came at all hours. Frankly, I was flattered that so many friends reached out. The attention didn't bother me at all. However, it made me aware that telling the same story over and over could be quite tiring.

When people go through, witness, or are close to a situation, especially one that's unique or traumatic, they can find themselves inundated with questions. Some are sincere, while others may be from people motivated only by a desire to gain inside information, have a vicarious experience of something sensational, or hear gory details.

Before long, the individual being asked "What happened?" can become exhausted, perhaps even questioning inquirers' motives. If we do sense that to be the case, whether the person is a close friend, co-worker, or casual acquaintance we encountered at the store, we should keep any inquisitive tendencies at bay.

As those who want to show love to our neighbor, it's up to us to keep this possibility in mind and do our best to discern when the need someone has for a listener is overshadowed by his or her need for privacy. We might just hear a statement of appreciation: "Thanks for not asking."

"You Can Observe A Lot By Watching." – Yogi Berra

The lofty neuroscience and scholarly research could lead us to conclude that noticing needs is complex. Fortunately, that's not the case. Regular people, like you and me, have everything it takes to notice needs.

Selective attention, the RAS, and reticular formation are useful tools. Conscious effort and practice can help. But toil and sweat are not required. Your desire to show love to others is enough.

Too often our bodies are in one place while our minds are somewhere else. In fact, sometimes our minds are not anywhere we know of. Have you ever been in your car, pulling into your neighborhood, with no memory at all of driving home?

These are the tendencies we must replace with our powers of observation. Keeping our eyes open and being aware is all we have to do. Because all around us there are needs.

Yogi Berra (1925-2015), the New York Yankees catcher as famous for his clever sayings as for his 19 years in the major leagues, expressed it well, even including it in the title to one of his books: *You Can Observe A Lot By Watching.*[7]

‒ ‒ ‒ ‒ ‒ ‒ ‒ ‒ ‒

Chapter Summary

You and I experience many social relations as we go through life. Most every person we meet has needs ranging from terribly sad, highly challenging problems, to the desire to share something positive and joyful.

Those who love people in practical ways are focused on the needs of the individual more than on the masses who have plenty. They leave the ninety-nine to connect with the one.

By realizing that the majority of people have some sort of need at any point in time, we will take conscious actions to notice those needs whenever we are in the presence of others.

We will do our best to be observant, practicing at first with our tangible surroundings, then focusing on people, looking at all the areas of human experience: physical, emotional, spiritual.

The very formation of the neurons in our brains will get involved. Through reticular formation, our reticular activating system will allow information about the needs of others to get our attention. We'll become masters in the art of detecting what's going on in the lives and minds of those around us.

Yogi Berra was right: Noticing needs is not at all complicated. And that's encouraging, because love notices the need.

Look Like You'll Make It

While you and I are busy noticing other people's needs, those same people are paying close attention to us as well. This presents a tremendous opportunity to set a positive example, and reminds me of a story from my own life.

In March 2013 I ran the Rock 'n' Roll Washington DC Marathon. Although my performance wasn't spectacular, something happened there that will stick with me always.

Running the 26.2 miles of a marathon is quite an experience. Elite athletes cover the course in a little over two hours. For the average Joe or Jill, four hours is good, and a time of five hours or more is quite common. Yeah, that is a lot of running. It can be daunting.

Moments after crossing the finish line that morning, a woman I had never met, who also just completed the event, tapped my shoulder. "Thank you so much," she exclaimed, giving me a hug. I had no idea what I'd done to deserve that, so I asked.

The woman explained that this was her first marathon, and she was afraid she wouldn't get to the end. She kept herself motivated by following me the entire way, beginning from the first few yards. "Why me?" I asked, to which she replied, "Because you looked like somebody who was going to make it."

Completing a marathon is never easy. But I had done it several times before and was sure I could do it that day. I'd trained hard, followed the advice of my coach, including a strict nutrition plan, and knew there was a group of friends back home, cheering. Indeed, both mental and physical struggles were involved. But I was determined to push through, and I guess it showed.

People's lives are filled with challenges. Their eyes and souls search the horizon for a stable harbor during storms of uncertainty. If you or I want to be the type of person who provides that stability, we will have to take some specific steps. Like training our minds to find the positives, nurturing our spirits, relying on past successes, engaging with a mentor, surrounding ourselves with the right influencers, and more.

Life is an endurance event. Despite its difficulties, let's do whatever's necessary so we can look like, and be, somebody who is going to make it.

6

Love Takes Action

No act of kindness, however small, is ever wasted.
– Aesop

Actions speak louder than words.
– Mom

Agnes Bojaxhiu was born in the city of Uskup (now Skopje, capital of Macedonia), on August 26, 1910. Her middle name, Gonxha, was derived from the Albanian word *Gonxhe*, which means "rosebud" or "little flower." Agnes' life did become a beautiful fragrance.

At the age of 18, Agnes left home to join the Sisters of Loreto in Ireland, a congregation of women dedicated to education. Three years later, she became a nun while continuing as a teacher of history and geography at St. Mary's High School, eventually rising to the position of headmistress.

Haunted by the poverty and suffering she observed, Agnes determined to give herself fully to the destitute. Over the remainder of her days, she left Europe and began a school for the poor, established a nursing home, a string of health facilities, an orphanage, and other efforts devoted to the needy, which she continued despite suffering a heart attack and the implantation of a pacemaker.

The world took notice. Agnes was awarded a Nobel Peace Prize and the United States Presidential Medal of Freedom, among other distinctions. In 2016, nineteen years after her death at the age of 87, Pope Francis posthumously declared her a saint.

Though all of Agnes' accomplishments were remarkable, her legacy is perhaps best remembered for founding the Missionaries of Charity, and for her work among lepers in India.

You may have heard of Agnes Gonxha Bojaxhiu by her more familiar name: Mother Teresa.[1]

— — — — — — — — — —

Love sees people as individuals. Love listens and asks questions. Love notices the need. And now we find that love takes action. Fortunately, this does not have to be at the level of Saint Mother Mary Teresa of Calcutta. Small deeds, rendered to single individuals, can be significant as well.

There's a famous quote by Henry David Thoreau which says, "the mass of men lead lives of quiet desperation." The word "quiet" signifies that people feel alone; cut off from others. A simple caring act, expressed in any of several ways, can break through, providing the sense that they're loved.

— — — — — — — — — —

Say What You See

One way to take action is to let the other person know what we observed. Noticing the need does little good if we keep silent about it. A few kind words of empathy can make a huge difference. The fact that another human acknowledges both our challenges and victories, and cares enough to comment, is taken as a significant act of love.

Saying, "You seem somewhat distracted today, is everything okay?" or "That's a nice tune you've been humming.

What brought it to your mind?" shows we see him or her as an individual with a story, not just a faceless object who is part of a transactional encounter.

Positive comments are appreciated also. Remarks such as "You really nailed your presentation at the sales meeting," or "The landscaping around your house is beautiful" or if appropriate, "That color looks fantastic on you," can light up a person's day. These go beyond compliments, although compliments are always welcome. The bigger significance is that by saying a few words we are taking an action. (In the context of this book, compliments that are flirtatious are not appropriate.)

Be careful when mentioning a person's appearance. It might at first seem empathetic to say, "Are you all right? You look tired." But what we might not know is that the person, despite fighting fatigue, went to great lengths to appear presentable. Hearing, "You look tired," could be deflating. Better to find some other way to show interest; maybe, "You seem deep in thought about something." If the person is overtired, you will probably uncover that, and the reasons why, soon enough.

As discussed previously, powerful listening happens when we find the other person's feelings and connect with them. This means paying attention to the emotions behind what is being said, then using words and phrases in our replies that show we picked up on those feelings.

People realize we have connected with their feelings when we say things like, "It must have made you sad to hear that news," (sad) … "I wouldn't be surprised if you're worried right now," (worried) … "That seems like a really amazing opportunity" (amazing).

Remember, also, to show appreciation when someone does a favor for you, extends a kindness in your direction, or makes a positive contribution to any area of your life. "Thank you. I really appreciate that. It meant a lot," goes a long way toward building bonds of closeness in a friendship. If you see something, be sure to speak up.

P.S. Or Not. In some situations, the best thing to say is nothing. People facing tough circumstances may want companionship, but not conversation. The quiet support of just being there can be a meaningful, highly loving way to take action. Don't feel that every second must be filled with words. Silence is sometimes even better. Be sensitive for times when it is appropriate to not say anything at all.

Small Can Be Enormous

Love takes action. But those actions don't have to be on a global scale. The thought of giving food to the hungry may conjure images of an international food bank using cargo jets to deliver pallets of canned goods and rice to remote parts of the world. While that's admirable, love is equally expressed by much smaller efforts.

I remember rushing to a meeting straight from the office one night, with no time for even a fast food drive through. I arrived famished. A young couple I met there said they had picked up turkey subs on the way to the meeting and it was buy two, get one free night, so they had an extra sandwich. Did I want it? Food for the hungry.

Once during a difficult transition in my life, a boss let me sleep on his sofa for a few weeks. Shelter for the wanderer.

(These examples are not meant to minimize the truly destitute who lack basic food or shelter. Organizations which meet needs at that level deserve our appreciation and support. Their actions are outside the scope of this book, however, which speaks to more everyday situations.)

An anthropologist, philosopher, and educator named Loren Eiseley (1907-1977) wrote an essay called "The Star Thrower," which has been adapted and retold thousands of times. It's the story of a young boy picking up starfish which were stranded on the beach when the tide went out, and throwing them back into the ocean. A man walks up and speaks to the boy, pointing out that there are miles of beach and hundreds of starfish, and there is no way that the youngster's efforts will make a difference. The boy bends down, picks up a starfish, tosses it into the surf and replies, "I made a difference for that one."

What a beautiful illustration of how each of us can take actions that make a difference, no matter how daunting the situation may seem.

How about the following?

—Paying for a co-worker's lunch at the cafeteria after noticing that he took the financial hit of an unexpected car repair this week.

—Offering to give someone a ride home from work, because that person usually walks to the bus stop and it's raining.

—Noticing that your spouse had a rough day, so telling him/her to relax while you clean up after dinner, even though that's a task the two of you normally share.

—Going next door to help an elderly neighbor put up hurricane shutters or shovel snow.

These acts, which may seem minor, can have huge ramifications. They are practical expressions of love. Small, perhaps, in comparison to the greatness of the need, but enormous to anyone who receives our acts of love.

Here's What I Can Do

When someone has a need, people often say, "Let me know if there's anything I can do." This is common following a job loss, after the death of a loved one, during an illness, when moving to a new home, and at other times in life.

Sadly, society has reduced, "Let me know if there's anything I can do," to a formality. So even for those who truly mean it, the offer gets lost in the clutter of insincere platitudes. Another problem with this statement is that it puts the burden on the person who needs the help. Many people find it difficult to reach out, even when, or maybe especially when, they are in a tough situation. Sometimes during a crisis, people are too distraught or exhausted to verbalize their needs.

While, "Let me know if there's anything I can do," shows good intentions, people rarely take anyone up on that generic offer.

There is an alternative which is more likely to result in an opportunity to take action. And with this approach, the actions we take will be less stressful for us and more beneficial to the person whose needs we are meeting. It involves giving thought to what the needs actually are (Chapter 5), then offering assistance in line with our strengths, or simply pitching in without even asking. If the need is there and we really can help, why ask? Just do it.

We each have unique talents and abilities, as well as those areas where we are not as proficient. Speaking personally, I wasn't born with the handyman gene. Suppose a friend is moving to a new home and I say the typical, "Let me know if there's anything I can do." I likely won't be asked to do anything at all. But if I did happen to be called upon to assemble furniture or hang pictures, that would probably not go well for either of us.

On the other hand, I can pick up boxes with the best of them, and I'm fully qualified to order pizza. So instead of "Let me know if there's anything I can do," it would be better all around if I said "I'll meet you at the new place in the morning and help carry stuff, then I'll bring lunch for the whole crew around noon."

A CPA buddy of mine guided a friend through the tax maze when her spouse passed away. Someone who loves to cook might provide meals to a sick neighbor. Reaching out to a busy couple with "I'd be glad to watch your kids so the two of you can have date night" is an excellent way to offer help if you enjoy baby-sitting. I consider myself a decent writer, so I often compose or proofread resumes and cover letters for job-seekers, or craft correspondence for people in sensitive predicaments.

If a friend just bought a new home, and you are an excellent painter, perhaps you could freshen up one of the bedrooms on a Saturday morning. Someone who loves landscaping could take care of the lawn for a neighbor with a broken leg. There are limitless opportunities.

Your actions to meet needs don't have to revolve around people's major life events. If you notice someone seems down or reclusive, instead of saying, "Tell me if you ever want to have lunch," you could say, "Let's go to lunch. I'll pick you up Saturday at 12:30." The same goes for acknowledging someone's good fortune. It can be "Meet me after work on Friday. We'll go out and celebrate," rather than simply "Feel free to call if you want to do anything."

When you propose a specific way to meet a need you've noticed, the offer is more likely to be accepted. And when the actions you take are in line with your unique strengths and abilities, everybody wins.

It's Not What You Know, It's Who You Know

Sometimes the best way to take an action that expresses love is to make an introduction. Mr. Chocolate, meet Mr. Peanut Butter. No one can meet every kind of need. We each have, however, a network of people who are knowledgeable in their own areas. Many of them would be willing to help if asked.

These introductions can meet needs on both sides of the equation. You may not be a contract attorney, but you may know a contract attorney. If you notice a colleague struggling with a problem in that area, your contribution might be to simply put the two in touch with one another. The person requiring the services gets what he or she needs, and your attorney friend gets a client or the opportunity for some fulfilling pro bono work.

Passing along a resume can help an unemployed person land a job, avoid financial ruin, meet obligations, and support a family. Equally, employers know how difficult it is to locate good candidates to join their firms. You just might receive a sincere "Thank you" from both of them.

Competent, honest auto mechanics are a valuable find. If you know one, that intro could benefit the person needing a car repair. No doubt, the shop owner will be appreciative as well.

This does not apply only to professions. Someone in need of a hobby to add enjoyment to life might like an introduction to the head of a bridge club. A colleague under doctor's orders to lose weight may welcome contact information for the fitness enthusiast you know. The possibilities are limited only by the number of people in your circle of acquaintances.

If we're serious about taking action to meet needs, we'll be deliberate about broadening our reach. Just as people in business work to expand their sphere of associates, be on the lookout for individuals who can jump in and take action to meet someone's need when you don't have the necessary skills yourself.

The next time you notice a need that is not in your personal wheelhouse, search your list for someone you know who could fill the gap. Then offer to make a match, or just go ahead and make it. Because who you know can be as valuable as what you know.

Introductions ... When To Be Careful

At times you may be tempted to introduce two people, because you have heard both of their stories and realize that one could help the other. Beware, as this could easily become a situation which looks as though you violated a confidence.

"Person A," a recovering gambling addict, could possibly help "Person B," who is struggling in that area. But neither of them may want the other to be aware of this part of their life. Perhaps the only safe way to proceed is to ask for and receive specific permission from both parties, without mentioning names or any details at all. You will simply refer to them as "someone who overcame this problem" and "someone who is facing this problem." Of course if either one does not wish to proceed, stop there.

Are You Speaking The Right Language?

Imagine saying the words "I love you" in English to someone who only understands French. The sentiment would be there, but the French-speaking person wouldn't receive the message. As obvious as that sounds, this same dilemma occurs in relationships all the time, and the people involved often are not even aware.

In his excellent book *The 5 Love Languages: The Secret to Love That Lasts*, author Gary Chapman explains that people express and receive love differently. While the book is primarily aimed at married couples, and is worth reading by every husband and wife, it applies to any interaction between people.

According to Chapman, the five love languages are:
—Words of affirmation.
—Gifts.
—Acts of service.
—Quality time.
—Physical touch (non-sexual).

To a "words of affirmation" guy, gifts are nice, but if someone really wants to warm his heart, a few accolades go a long way. In a marriage, he might long for his wife to say she thinks he is a good provider, that the outdoor barbecue he built is magnificent, or that she really appreciates his efforts to connect with the kids. At work, "Well done," from the boss makes his day—the more often and specific, the better. And in a friendship, acknowledgments of his many good qualities and his positive personal development will be extremely meaningful.

At the same time, Mr. Words Of Affirmation must not assume those around him primarily feel loved in the same way he does. This is a common mistake leading to misunderstandings and hurt feelings.

A "words of affirmation" type could compliment a "quality time" person repeatedly, but if he or she doesn't hang out with that person, what is meant as a message of love will fall short. Instead, they will need to spend time together. That might mean tagging along while taking the dog for a walk, watching a movie, having a conversation about a current event, or something similar.

To express love in ways that are meaningful to someone, we will want to make sure we know the person's love language and are taking action accordingly. Obviously, this pertains mainly to those with whom we have ongoing relationships. Co-workers, neighbors, people who share our interests, spouses and other family members are prime candidates.

Like so many other things we do to express love, our attempts don't have to be huge. "Gifts" can be a card, a cupcake from the bakery, or a book you found at the thrift store. "Acts of service" could be helping wash someone's car or offering to pick up dog food when you're headed to the pet supply store after work. A sincere arm around the shoulder, or pat on the back can be "physical touch," if that's appropriate in the relationship.

Once we know people's preferences, we can tailor our energies accordingly. This ensures we are "speaking" the right language, so the message of love comes through.

The 5 Love Languages: The Secret to Love That Lasts, by Dr. Gary Chapman, has sold over five million copies and been translated into 38 languages. It's a valuable book for anyone who wants to love his or her neighbor in practical ways.

Tools In The Shed

As you and I go through life, we pick up inspirational sayings, bits of wisdom, techniques, favorite books and articles, processes, core values—life hacks of all types. After a few years, a person who is observant, curious, and desirous to learn can wind up with a significant collection of these. We can think of them as tools for navigating life.

A physical tool like a battery-powered drill is not used every day, but when we need one, nothing else will do and we're glad to have it. Likewise, certain life situations require just the right tool; perhaps a system for making sure we don't forget important birthdays, time management techniques, spiritual quotes that bring strength during difficulties, ideas for stretching the budget—the possibilities go on. When certain circumstances appear, having the right solution available can help us tackle them confidently.

To ensure we can lay our hands on a particular wrench, screwdriver or power drill, we keep them in a special place such as a storage shed. Our life tools need to be kept somewhere as well, so we don't have to remember them all. An actual list on paper or in some digital application is a good idea. It can be as simple or complex as you want. The objective is to be able to retrieve one of these life tools when a situation calls for it.

Make it a point to acquire as many life tools as possible. Keep your eyes and ears open, read great literature, consult with mentors, and note what successful people do. When you notice what someone is going through in life, take a trip to the metaphorical storage shed where your tools are kept and pull out an appropriate one. Then share it with the person who has a need.

What tools do you already have in your shed? Probably more than you think. Take inventory and work at finding more. You'll wind up with another effective way to show love by taking action.

As We Were Saying ...

An excellent action to take is this: follow up. In other words, get back to people at some future date after an initial interaction.

Situations to follow up could include medical tests, job interviews, important meetings, time-sensitive matters, victories to celebrate, good or bad news the person was anticipating, difficult experiences, matters about people's children, and more.

Asking for an update the next time you're with that person is tremendous. Perhaps even more meaningful is to reach out between get-togethers for the specific purpose of checking in with someone.

Your follow up might be to gain information by asking questions such as "How did it go?" or "What happened in that phone call you had to make?" Or it could involve digging for the person's feelings, with inquiries like "How are you holding up after what you went through?"

Making some additional contribution a few hours, days, or weeks after the original discussion, such as sharing an article or other relevant tidbit, is another good way to follow up. This is an excellent use of the tools in your shed.

If you are a friend to several people, it can be difficult to keep track of everything going on in their lives. Don't be ashamed to make a list on paper or set reminders in your digital calendar. It doesn't make your actions less sincere to have a little outside-the-brain assistance.

Follow up. Then notice how impressed people will be, and how they feel warmly touched when you take action this way. It's a tremendous expression of love.

– – – – – – – – –

Chapter Summary

Love takes action. After seeing every person as an individual with a story, intently listening to those stories, asking questions to learn more, and noticing the need, love does something to help. This doesn't have to be a monumental, global undertaking. (Though it could be.) We won't all become the next Mother Teresa.

Verbal acknowledgments of the needs we have noticed are an easy way to take action. If we see something, we should usually speak up about it.

Even small efforts can be significant. Paying for a friend's lunch, giving someone a ride to work, inviting a coworker to spend an evening with you when you notice he or she seems lonely; these are all excellent ways to take action and express love.

We each have unique gifts and talents. Rather than extending the generic "Let me know if there's anything I can do," it's better to offer to help in a way that reflects your talents, or to just jump in and do it.

In situations where we don't have the skills required to meet a need, we might know someone who does. Making an introduction between the one in the situation, and a person who specializes in that area can be a godsend to both parties. Who you know can be as helpful as what you know.

People perceive they are loved in different ways. Dr. Gary Chapman wrote a book about this called *The 5 Love Languages: The Secret to Love That Lasts.* Understanding these distinct perspectives, then making efforts to apply the ones most significant to each individual will go a long way toward making people feel loved.

As we go through life, we pick up techniques for dealing with various situations. We find solutions to common problems, hear motivational sayings, collect anecdotes that reveal wisdom, and more. We can store these in what could be thought of as a sort of tool shed full of resources which will be helpful to others at specific times. When the relevant need comes up, we'll be ready.

Following up with people after an initial contact to get an update or provide additional input is hugely significant. Making lists can help.

In all these ways and more, we have equipped ourselves to fulfill a critical element of practical love. We are poised to take action.

A Twist On Regifting

I once received a tin of popcorn around Christmas. (It wasn't really a tin of popcorn. I changed that detail in case the person who gave it to me reads this.)

Rarely do I eat popcorn, but I knew someone who enjoyed it, so I passed the goodies her way, unopened and with the ribbon still intact. She was very appreciative, and no one was aware of my secret. Later I learned there is a word for this: regifting. What's more, I was informed that this was a bad move on my part because, so I'm told, people are not supposed to do that.

My personal opinion on regifting physical items doesn't matter. But there is another type of regifting that is worth a little more consideration.

Each of us has been given gifts of the non-tangible kind. We call them talents, knacks, proficiencies, aptitudes, and a few other words and phrases. And here is the kicker—these competencies were not meant to be kept to ourselves. They are for the benefit of people around us.

We have an obligation to pass those unique abilities of ours on to others in need. It's another way to live out the truth that love takes action. I can't imagine anyone will complain, and we can do this kind of regifting all year long.

7

Love Speaks The Truth

Is it true; is it kind, or is it necessary?
– Socrates

In a letter to a group of people professing to be devoted to one another, the writer told them with some authority to be sure they were "speaking the truth in love." What does that mean?

The phrase "speaking the truth in love" may need some explaining. After all, those words were written a few thousand years ago, and modern humans communicate differently. Perhaps it makes more sense to say, "speak the truth, and do it in a loving manner."

Next, we want to unpack what it means to speak the truth. Is the truth the same as what we are feeling in the moment, or is it more objective than that? There are moral absolutes, but beyond those it may not always be possible to know the truth, especially when it comes to the direction for another person's life. Could it be that attempting to speak the truth to someone requires a large dose of humility?

And what does it mean to speak in a loving manner? Words such as patient, kind, honoring, humble, gracious, and fair come to mind. These are wonderful sentiments, but if we are seething with anger, a loving conversation probably won't take place. So there may be some personal preparation and timing considerations involved.

People sometimes want to be "right" for no reason other than to boost their own egos. While this may provide temporary satisfaction, it comes at the expense of connection.

Truth spoken in a loving manner has the power to help someone grow or avoid making a serious mistake. Mastering this art is worth every effort.

A Balancing Act

Since there are two elements to be considered—truth and love— there are at least two ways we can get out of balance. We can fail to speak the truth at all, or we can speak the truth but fail to do it in a loving manner.

There can be reluctance for people to share observations and insights that are truthful, reasonable, and would be helpful to the hearer. The concern is they might offend the person by stating something potentially difficult to hear. So they don't say anything at all, believing they are holding back in the name of love.

On the surface, this seems to make sense. But there are flaws in the logic. First, to let people remain oblivious to their effects on others, or to silently watch them make unwise, possibly dangerous choices, is less than loving. Secondly, the position stems from a false assumption that delivering difficult news is always a negative experience for everyone involved. We call it "confrontation," and people avoid it like the plague. Thankfully, confrontations can be far from the horrible experiences we dread, as we will soon discover.

The flip side happens when someone has no hesitation about speaking what he or she deems to be truth but does it in an unloving way. These folks see nothing wrong with hitting someone head on with whatever message they feel is necessary, no matter how harsh the delivery. "It is what it is," they say. "I have to speak the truth, or I wouldn't be showing love." Umm, not so.

Neither of these positions fulfill what it means to speak the truth in love. We can do better.

— — — — — — — — — —

A Friday Afternoon With Jennifer

My relationship with Jennifer had several facets. (Sadly, this remarkable woman died in December 2018, at the young age of 66. A tragic loss to the world.)

It started when Jennifer and the company she owned signed on as a client of the marketing and advertising agency I was running at the time. Because Jennifer's firm taught presentation skills, I soon became a client of hers, giving us a reciprocal business association. And through those frequent interactions, a personal friendship developed.

One Friday morning, Jennifer called. "I want to see you this afternoon to discuss some changes to my website," she said. It was last minute, and my calendar was already tight, but a project from a paying customer took priority. We arranged to meet in her office at 4:00 p.m.

For the first 15 minutes, the discussion covered ways that my company could further improve her corporation's online presence. Then Jennifer opened the credenza and pulled out a bottle of wine, some cheese, and walnuts. Placing them on the table at which we were sitting, she said, "I think you and I have worked enough for one week. How about we have a friendly talk now. Is that alright with you?" I agreed.

"It's occurred to me that you might be just the slightest bit critical," Jennifer stated with a grin. "I've noticed a tendency from you in that direction. I'm wondering if you sense any truth to this, and if so, how that might be affecting your family, your marriage, friendships and the business." Then she smiled fully— that huge smile I had seen often, which lit up her eyes—and took a sip of a fine Italian red.

Over the next two hours or so, Jennifer and I had a glorious conversation, as well as some good refreshments. She asked questions, listened, told me her observations, and helped me think through them. In response, I was able to share honestly. The discoveries about myself, and lessons I learned that day are still with me, several years later. My life improved as a result. And there were many other times like this with my dear friend.

Here was a person who knew how to speak the truth, and do it in a loving manner.

Confrontation? Please No! (But It's Not That Bad.)

The idea of "confrontation" sends many people running for the exits. Most of us resist the thought of confronting. Just mention the topic and you'll hear "I avoid confrontation," "I hate to confront" or "I've never been good at confronting."

Thinking of confrontation brings up visions of an awkward meeting in a cold setting. We remember being sent to the principal's office, the "Wait until your father gets home" scenario, and "The boss wants to see you right away."

Trepidation also occurs when we are the one initiating the confrontation. We anticipate defensiveness, an argument, or rejection of our points. We fear the other person will lash back, releasing pent up criticisms at us in return.

Either way, we just know there will be shouting involved and when it's over, the parties on both sides of the discussion will be further apart than when the conversation began. No wonder we dislike confrontation!

It's time to discover a new way of thinking. We'll find that confrontations don't have to be scary at all. In fact, like my Friday afternoon with Jennifer, they can be pleasant.

What's In A Word?

According to the Online Etymology Dictionary,[1] a website that publishes word origins, the term "confrontation" came into common usage in the 1630s. Its meaning at the time was "the action of bringing two parties face to face." There was nothing adversarial about it. This same source also states that the negative idea of confrontation began with the Cuban missile crisis of 1962.

Take a moment and try to wipe out everything you ever thought about confrontations. Now imagine that instead of thinking, "I have to confront my friend," you think, "I'm going to get face to face with my friend." And forget the intimidating environment like the office of an authority figure. This face-to-face conversation can happen at a park or over dinner. What's more, you will be saying what's on your mind in a sensitive, caring way, which will make it even less fearful for you both.

The idea of face to face also implies that both parties get to express what's on their minds. (They both have faces after all.) This should lessen the pressure. It's not one hundred percent up to you to take the event from A to Z. It's a collaboration.

Face-to-face meeting. Loving dialogue. Both parties participating. Confronting doesn't seem so bad now, does it?

You might look forward to a get together like that.

A mindset shift around confrontation could revolutionize our lives. Learning to view confronting as the positive act of meeting someone face to face with the objective of speaking truth in love will improve our relationships, reduce our stress levels, and make us better able to love our neighbor in practical ways.

Preparing To Confront

There you are, face to face with another person. You're ready to bring up an important topic. The insights you plan to share are based on observations, enhanced by experience. You feel certain the conversation will be beneficial to the other person, leading to his or her personal growth or the avoidance of a negative consequence. You are fully convinced that what you have to say represents truth, and you plan to share it in a loving way.

Still, the message could be difficult for the person to hear. That's why you prepared thoroughly by studying a few guidelines to help the confrontation go smoothly.

Guidelines For Speaking The Truth In Love Through Confrontation

Envision The Big Picture

Before arranging a time to get together, ask yourself a few questions about how you see the confrontation playing out. What are your true motives? What do you hope to accomplish? What would a positive outcome look like? Do you plan to present your concern and leave it at that, or will you push for an admission, commitment, or some other specific response? Have you factored in time for the other person to speak, so it doesn't become one-way communication? Are you prepared to stay calm, or even walk away, if things take a turn for the worse?

What is your general attitude about this person and the situation? Confronters who consider themselves crusaders for righteousness, with a mission to set another person straight, are dangerous. These interactions usually head downhill quickly, becoming arguments rather than face-to-face discussions.

On the other hand, entering a face-to-face meeting with only the other person's best interests in mind will often lead to mutual understanding, and closer bonds of friendship.

Ask Permission

It's best to ask permission before opening a sensitive conversation. Saying "I've noticed something I think would be good for us to discuss. Is that okay with you?" or a similar question works well. Generally the person will say "Sure," and you can proceed.

If he or she doesn't want to go there, you should respect that. Unless the situation is severe, you have done your part, and can continue to be a friend in all the other ways explored in this book.

Consider the timing of the confrontation as well. When people are tired, preoccupied, or have other demands pressing, they are less receptive to a deep interaction. So even if you are together at the moment, ask if it's convenient to talk right then or if he or she would prefer to put a meeting on the calendar. Short of emergencies, whatever you have to say can wait.

If you do receive permission to move ahead, the conversation can continue.

Check Your Emotions

The way we express our emotions can build or damage a relationship.

We don't want to direct negative emotions at the other person as if he or she is the cause of the way we feel. This isn't a matter of "I'm so disappointed because of your behavior." It's simply a statement of our observations and insights.

Anger, channeled properly, has its place in healthy relationships, and may be a valid part of what prompts someone to confront. But be careful not to view confrontation as an excuse to vent your anger in a rude, hurtful way. Speaking the truth in love is not a license to get something off your chest. Although clearing the slate is usually good, uncontrolled anger is unlikely to produce compassionate interaction.

Take care not to project your own emotional concerns that have nothing to do with the other person. You may have had a frightening experience while traveling in a foreign country. That doesn't mean, however, that you should let your fear take over, expressing displeasure if your adult son or daughter decides to plan a family trip to Europe.

Of course emotions which are expressed properly can bring people closer. As discussed previously, always look for and try to find and connect with the person's feeling. If he or she is excited, sad, depressed, elated, or whatever the case, reflect back in a way which shows you get it and are willing to join the person in that emotion. This adds to a loving confrontation and strengthens the connection between you.

Be Straightforward

Permission received and emotions in check, state the reason for the confrontation in a straightforward way. No accusations or beating around the bush. No metaphors. No comparisons. Just describe what's on your mind. Then give the person a chance to respond. This will encourage a true conversation rather than an accusation session.

So don't say "I've heard you talk about taking on a payment for a new car, yet you've told me you can barely cover rent. That's irresponsible." And don't say "David handles his finances so well. Why can't you be like him?"

But you might say "I notice you've been talking about buying a new car. A few weeks ago you told me the budget was tight. How are you viewing your financial picture overall?" This option gives the other person a chance to explain his or her point of view. It's a face-to-face discussion, not a one-sided monologue.

Do Your Best To Understand

In his best-selling book, *The 7 Habits Of Highly Effective People*, author Stephen R. Covey advises us to work toward understanding others before asking them to understand us. This is a tremendous objective to have during a confrontation.

Before launching into all the irrefutable (in your estimation) truths you want the other person to know, be sure you fully grasp what's on his or her mind. Phrases such as "Please clarify that a little more for me" or "Help me understand what you're saying" will move the conversation in that direction.

It can be valuable to repeat back to the person what you think he or she wishes to communicate. Perhaps state something like "Just to be sure we're on the same page, let me tell you what I heard you say, and then you can tell me if I got it."

Once you are fully clear on what the other person wants you to know, you can move forward by sharing your thoughts. This will usually build a bridge of understanding.

Stay On Topic

A more recent definition of confronting that may help guide your time with another person is this: "Confronting means pointing out inconsistencies between what a person is doing and what that person says he or she is doing."

Ask yourself what the person is doing that differs from his or her words or the image he or she projects. Let only that be the topic of your confrontation. Avoid any temptation to let the discussion drift into other areas, such as "There was also that day when …" or "Your brother even says you …"

Sometimes a person will try to sidestep the current issue with something ancillary. If you see this happening, politely suggest that the other matter be addressed later. Then get the discussion back on track.

Set Aside Your Pet Peeves

Pet peeves can color the way we approach an interaction. Maybe we value promptness and see tardiness as disrespectful no matter the reason. If we let personal opinions such as these shape how we speak, there is a greater chance of things not going well. Better to enter the conversation in an open-minded, truth-seeking manner before we get carried away. There could be valid reasons the person is habitually late, and it's not a lack of respect at all.

Or perhaps we need to just set aside our pet peeve and put up with that annoyance, making an allowance for it. (See Chapter 8.)

Avoid Value Judgments

If the situation you are confronting is about a definite legal or moral violation, you'll have to address it as such. Those situations are likely outside the scope of this book. A therapist or other professional may be able to give advice on how to handle them.

The type of confrontations we will be entering will usually involve behaviors which are simply less than ideal or likely to result in negative consequences. Be careful not to project right vs. wrong judgments on these. Saying "This behavior was bad, and the alternative would have been good" will likely get you shut out.

People are so accustomed to being judged that they expect it to happen. If you imply there are clear right and wrong paths, they will typically conclude that you think they are on the path that's wrong. On the other hand, people are more likely to examine themselves when they don't feel judged.

There is always the possibility that our assessments could miss the mark. And even if we're dead on, unless the other person sees it for him or herself, the lessons are not likely to stick.

Don't Assume Motives ... Instead, Be Curious

It is virtually impossible to know what drives another human being's actions, so be cautious about making assumptions. Assuming to have a person's motives figured out by saying something like "You were trying to get Alex in trouble when you told Will that Alex was late for work twice this week" is likely to start an argument, and you may be incorrect anyway. It's better to ask rather than presume to have insights you simply can't possess.

"Why" questions may not be the best approach, as they could easily put the other person on the defensive. Imagine being asked "Why did you do that?" Even with good intentions, it can seem like an accusation.

Instead, a question such as "What do you think was behind your decision?" comes across much softer and gives the other person an opportunity to explain in what feels like a safer environment.

Don't Seek To Punish Or Assign Blame

Conversations are sometimes used to punish an individual for what looked to us like a poor decision. We convince ourselves we're pursuing fairness or justice, so severe words or attitudes are warranted. But the shortcomings of others don't matter if our own shortcoming is to treat them with a lack of love.

If the person's behavior resulted in negative consequences to him/herself or another person, it's easy to assign blame. This isn't necessary and seldom helps. Some individuals are mature enough to take responsibility for their actions without being prompted. On the other hand, people who are prone to sidestepping responsibility will do that no matter how much evidence you present. Speak the truth in love, and let the person take it from there.

Select Your Words Carefully

Stay away from disparaging words and phrases which attack the other person's worth as a human. You're discussing actions, not core character. A specific choice may have been irresponsible, but that doesn't necessarily mean you are speaking with an irresponsible person. Either way, it's not your place to draw that conclusion.

The terms "never" and "always" should be avoided, because they are seldom true, and can cause people to feel defeated and without hope.

Remain Humble

Human nature is universal. Psychologists state that the very fact we see faults in others suggests those same faults exist within ourselves. So when we confront, we need to be equally truthful internally, acknowledging that we too are weak, susceptible to all types of shortcomings, and quite likely in need of loving confrontation as well.

It's said that Michelangelo inscribed the words "*ancora imparo*," which means "I am still learning," on a sketch at the age of 87. I can't vouch for that (and there's debate around it), but Jennifer—who I mentioned at the beginning of this chapter, and was one of the wisest people I ever met—had the letters "IaSL" after her name on her business card. When people asked her what this meant, she cheerfully quoted the same thing: "I am still learning."

Nobody is free from faults or knows it all, so stay humble.

And Just The Same …

Suppose the other person accepts what you have to say, expresses a degree of remorse, or makes a commitment to change as the result of a confrontation. Even then, there are factors which could still cause the relationship to be harmed. Perhaps you somehow violated one of the guidelines in this chapter, or maybe you did everything right and he or she had a negative reaction, nonetheless.

If you sense a strain between you and the other person after a confrontation, examine the reason for it and seek another face-to-face meeting. Let the person know that your goal is to restore the relationship or make it even stronger than it was before. Then use what you learned to make the next discussion turn out better.

But don't worry; what's more likely is that your confrontations will be beneficial and result in significant steps toward loving your neighbor.

Whose Idea Is It Anyway?

At times, we really do have a clear picture of what would be the best course of action for someone to take. (Though I maintain it's nearly impossible to know for sure.) Even so, it is best not to state those thoughts too forcefully.

The more effective route, usually, is to keep your comments focused on the person's actions, and their past, current, or likely outcomes. Speak to the reality of the situation, not your opinion of it. Your opinion may be correct, but unless people make discoveries on their own, the insights will have a much lower impact.

Some face-to-face meetings will be about an upcoming decision. Maybe your nephew is thinking of leaving a stable job to chase a risky scheme, and you've seen this cycle in his life several times before. Unless you have been specifically asked for input, it is probably best to stay neutral on what you think he should do, even if you have a solid recommendation in mind. You can ask questions, make sure he's pondered this or that angle, explore whether this direction dovetails with other goals of his family, and the like. If he does open the door, lovingly state your thoughts, but he will have to make the final decision himself.

People need to be self-motivated, not pressured externally, even if the voice coming from the outside has their best interests in mind. They need to feel that the ideas they follow are theirs, not someone else's.

Open the conversation, have a dialogue, and leave it

there. Honor the person's right to make decisions for his or her own life, then be at peace. You did your part.

What About The Sandwich?

One technique which has made the rounds, especially in business, is what is called a "criticism sandwich." You might be familiar with it. A criticism sandwich begins with a compliment, then states the problem, then ends with another compliment. The two bookend positives are supposed to soften the blow of the negative in the middle.

While the criticism sandwich has many fans, it also has serious downsides. People on the receiving end often see through it as an obvious gimmick. They may feel patronized, and the compliments can get lost in the resentment of being manipulated.

The criticism sandwich is much more transactional than relational. It is a hit and run approach that puts control in the hands of the speaker, with little opportunity for dialogue. And it runs contrary to our understanding of confrontation; we're not criticizing, we're having a face-to-face discussion.

There may be room in the workplace for the criticism sandwich (or there may not), but it's not recommended as a way to speak the truth in love. It's a tactic that could be construed as insincere.

— — — — — — — — —

Chapter Summary

Love speaks the truth. This requires some explanation, because of misconceptions about what the phrase "speaking the truth in love" means. A clearer way to think of this is that our goal is to speak the truth, and to do so in a loving manner.

Speaking the truth in love is helped significantly by an understanding of what it means to confront. This is not the scary experience modern word usage implies. Traced to its roots from the 1630s, "confrontation" simply means "bringing two parties face to face."

Successful confrontations require a bit of advance preparation.

We first think about the big picture of the confrontation, asking ourselves questions about our motives, goals, desired outcomes, and more.

It's usually best to ask the other person's permission for a face-to-face meeting. If there is reluctance, don't proceed.

There are effective and ineffective ways to express emotions during a confrontation. Becoming familiar with those, and acting accordingly, is critical.

Be straightforward, and as Stephen R. Covey advised, do your best to understand the other person before you ask him or her to understand you.

Express your thoughts compassionately, without cute techniques, condescension, comparisons, or criticisms. Allow the person to help you understand his or her point of view. And stay on topic, not letting the discussion drift into other areas.

Set aside any pet peeves, and avoid value judgments and assumptions about motives. Instead, be curious. If you don't understand what was behind someone's actions, simply ask.

Don't seek to punish, or place blame. Let the other person accept whatever level of responsibility he or she feels is appropriate.

Select your words carefully, staying away from character attacks and the words "always" and "never" which deflate hope and denote defeat.

Knowing the frailties of human nature, including our own, remain humble. We have shortcomings as well, and are still learning.

Sometimes the person will make changes as a result of a loving confrontation. That's more likely if the motivation comes from within him or her, not from someone else's suggestion. Once we share our thoughts, we let others decide what is right for their own lives.

Criticism sandwich? If effective at all, it should be saved for the workplace. In a friendship (and maybe even on the job) this can seem patronizing or manipulative.

With all these bases covered, you are far more likely to speak the truth, and do so in a loving manner. That's what love does.

Face To Face Can Be Side By Side

The reason for a confrontation, which means bringing two parties face to face, is to get them to share openly, in an atmosphere of acceptance. Ironically, this sometimes works best when the parties are not face to face, but side by side.

I have warm memories of standing side by side at the kitchen sink in the days before owning an electric dishwasher. The first of those memories are from my youth. I can't say the conversations were profound, but the laughter and love were apparent as Mom washed, I dried, and my big brother put away, because he could reach the top shelf. Later in life, my wife Linda and I mulled over several topics in a similar kitchen venue early in our marriage. We also hosted large group dinners where friendships deepened as we performed clean up duty together.

Who hasn't had a meaningful discussion riding side by side in a car? Or how about sharing from the recesses of our souls while sitting on a park bench? Taking a walk, or going for a run if the two are so inclined, can provide an ideal opportunity to connect.

In all these side-by-side environments, humans do some of their most reflective sharing. They reveal things that would rarely get shared anywhere else.

Side by side, it's a great way to be face to face.

8

Love Makes Allowances

When you stop expecting
people to be perfect, you can
like them for who they are.
– Donald Miller

Being a first timer at a running club is interesting. One personal example taught me something about making allowances for others.

The scheduled workout was a four-mile loop through a park I'd never visited before. Everyone else was a regular at this weekly event, and familiar with the route, but I didn't know it at all. A young lady sensed this and asked if I needed a running buddy for the evening. I replied, "Yes." She asked how fast I wanted to go, and I told her: ten minutes, thirty seconds per mile. "No problem," she responded and off we went. I noticed we were trailing behind the rest of the group, but as I'm a bit older than most runners, that wasn't unusual.

Returning to home base, one of the other participants wanted to know what our pace had been. When I told him, he turned to the woman with whom I had been running and asked, "Can you even run that slow?"

Although my companion just smiled, it was then I learned she was a local elite athlete who often won races in the area. Without me holding her back, she would have been clipping off those four miles under seven minutes each, which is a huge difference from what we had been doing. But for the new guy, me, she made an allowance.

– – – – – – – – – –

Can't Get Around It

Making allowances for others is a critical element for loving our neighbors. Without this it is nearly impossible to show love to anyone for long. That's because people are not always easy to love. Allowances are necessary to grease the rough spots between us. There's no getting around it.

I've thought now and then of how peaceful the world would be if everyone were exactly like me. I hope you just chuckled. Obviously, this would create disaster. But it would make MY life easier, so it seems. I would know exactly how people would behave in every situation and why. They would do things in ways that make perfect sense to me. (Though sometimes I don't even make sense to myself.)

Human beings' tastes vary. One person likes things neat and orderly. Someone else thrives on chaos. There are people who get straight to the point in a conversation, and those who ramble on about every detail. Topics as simple as what type of movie people prefer to watch, the best temperature for the air conditioner, and where to squeeze the toothpaste tube can all challenge our resolve to show love. (No. Scratch that. There's only ONE right way to squeeze the toothpaste tube.)

Here are a few more situations that force us to exercise our ability to make allowances:

—It takes her forever to put on makeup.
—His desk is so messy! I don't see how he knows where anything is.
—Every time we agree to meet somewhere, they show up late.
—She's sarcastic.

—His political ideas are way different from mine.

—There's trash all over the interior of his car.

—Their children are allowed to run wild.

And those are examples of mere personal preference. What about behaviors that are more universally annoying? Things like poor grooming, embarrassing habits, not doing a fair share of the chores, language that's inappropriate for the situation. It can be even tougher to make allowances for those.

Yes, some people rub us the wrong way. They get under our skin. Our irritation might be justified, or the things that bug us could be just matters of opinion. Either way, if we're serious about loving our neighbor, we have to do something about this. Usually that means making allowances.

Mind The Gap

Another aspect of human psychology will help us understand why it is sometimes difficult to make allowances. In fact, a thorough grasp on this concept might even turn us into allowance-making experts. This one has to do with ways to look at and display empathy. (Empathy definition: The ability and/or capacity to feel what another person is feeling, and/or experience what another person is experiencing.)

Dr. George Loewenstein, a professor at Carnegie Mellon University, coined the phrase "Hot-Cold Empathy Gap." Loewenstein teaches that when people who are not presently in a particular situation predict how they think they would act in that situation, those predictions are generally different from the way they do act when they are actually in that situation. (You might need to read that last sentence another time or two. It's a mouthful.)

The hot-cold empathy gap takes into consideration the different environments in which someone finds him or herself. These environments are labeled as either a hot state or a cold state.

For example, a person who is not hungry (cold state) and is thinking about what to order at a restaurant for dinner later that evening, may fully believe that he or she will choose a salad. Once at the restaurant and feeling hungry (hot state), that person is likely to order a bacon double cheeseburger and fries without thinking about it. In the words of psychologists, the behavior was "state dependent," and there was a gap between the decisions that were anticipated in the cold state vs. those made in the hot state.

People who are in cold states—such as calm, rested, sexually fulfilled, emotionally stable, feeling secure, at peace—might think they know what they would do in a particular situation. But when those same people are in a hot state—anger, fatigue, arousal, depression, anxiety, fear—what they actually do in that situation can be far different from what they previously envisioned. And those are just a few of the many hot-cold drivers.

The hot-cold empathy gap associated with state-dependent behaviors can be either intrapersonal or interpersonal. The first, inTRApersonal, describes gaps in the empathy we give ourselves. The inTERpersonal are empathy gaps between us and others.

Intrapersonal Hot-Cold Empathy Gaps

A lack of intrapersonal empathy, empathy expressed toward ourselves, occurs when we are back in a cold state and beating ourselves up over how we acted in a hot state. We're angry with ourselves for choosing the burger and fries, when we were sure we would order a salad. Or for raising our voice during a sensitive discussion when we made a personal promise an hour before that we would keep our emotions under control.

Interpersonal Hot-Cold Empathy Gaps

Interpersonal hot-cold empathy gaps, empathy gaps between us and others, occur because when you are in a cold state, it's virtually impossible to understand why another person acted a certain way when he or she was in a hot state. Someone whose stomach is full after a healthy meal (cold state) is incapable of knowing all the pressures which influenced someone else to have a 3,000-calorie burger and fries when that other person was famished and the food was just a quick order away (hot state).

The person who was unpleasant, the one who replied sarcastically, the neighbor who acted grumpy—what underlying hot state factors were at play when those situations occurred? It might be arrogant, and is surely less than loving, to sit in our cold state armchairs and draw conclusions as to the type of people those individuals are, and then to treat them less lovingly.

If we're ignorant of this psychological concept, we may fall prey to a serious gap in the empathy we show toward others; a hot-cold empathy gap. On the other hand, understanding this will help us make allowances and show love to our neighbor.

Nobody's Perfect — Not Even Me

Everyone has quirks, idiosyncrasies, even flat-out faults. That includes me. That includes you.

It's difficult to admit that the person in the mirror possesses shortcomings just like everyone else. Perhaps a dose of humility would be helpful, realizing that other people are likely making allowances for us.

A business consultant gave a presentation about relationships in the workplace. "Close your eyes," she told the participants, "and create a mental picture of the face of a coworker who irritates the bejeebers out of you." After ten or 15 seconds she said, "Now, please rest assured that there is someone in this room who, in his or her mind, at this very moment, is envisioning a picture of you."

While the story is amusing, it underscores a truth. Nobody is perfect. That is another good reason to make allowances.

Looking Behind The Curtain

We might be more prone to make allowances if we remember one of the first points explored in this book: everybody has a story. Many times that story will provide insights as to why someone acts as he or she does.

—The person who speaks louder than necessary may have been raised with a houseful of noisy siblings. The only way to be heard was to speak up.

—The one who's a control freak might have been the oldest of four children with a father in prison and a mom working two jobs. Somebody had to take charge.

—The co-worker who lashes out when questioned was perhaps abused as a powerless, vulnerable child. She's never told anyone or dealt with the trauma. "Nobody's going to treat me like that again," she vowed, and reacts accordingly when she feels backed into a corner.

—The colleague who rarely reaches for the check at lunch remembers watching his mother count change to buy groceries. He has a scarcity mentality, fearing that the future is insecure.

There can even be medical reasons for behaviors we find odd. Hyperacusis is a hearing disorder which makes it hard for some people to deal with everyday sounds. A noise that is perfectly acceptable to you may startle someone else. This is just one example of many.

Understanding what's beneath the surface can soften our attitudes. We may then find it easier to make the allowances which are so important to showing love to others.

We Can't Always Explain

People also have weaknesses which can NOT be explained. One person becomes a basket case in the face of anything remotely dangerous. Another is hugely uncomfortable in a crowd. Some men and women have a difficult time expressing themselves verbally. They may not be able to explain why.

These mysteries do not exempt people from the consequences of their actions. They do, however, present an additional opportunity for you and me to make allowances.

Mercy And Grace

Making allowances for others will require an understanding of mercy and grace. The two are related, but not the same.

Mercy means we are spared some or all of the negative consequences we should have had to suffer. Grace happens when we receive some act of consideration that goes above what we deserve.

When a police officer stops a speeding driver and doesn't issue a citation, it's mercy. The driver should have gotten a ticket and did not. If the officer were to stop someone who was going within the speed limit and present the person behind the wheel with a hundred-dollar bill, that would be grace. Obeying the law doesn't usually come with a reward, but in this case it did.

Someone clearly does something offensive. We feel angry. We want to give him or her a piece of our mind, point out the error, and state in no uncertain terms our personal formula for how the situation should have been handled. We refrain, however, and stay silent, or express ourselves in a kind, caring way. That's mercy.

At other times, we might exhibit grace. A classic example is being at a party with a friend who is a recovering alcoholic. If you're not tempted to excess drinking yourself, it would be okay to have a beer, a glass of wine, or a cocktail. But if you don't drink any alcohol at all that evening, so as not to create an awkward situation for your friend who might be struggling, that's an act of grace.

Looking at these traits from the reverse angle, dishing out every bit of punishment we feel a mistake demands is the ultimate lack of mercy. Holding people to impossibly high standards shows an extreme lack of grace.

—Mercy = sparing someone from negative consequences.
—Grace = acts of consideration that go beyond what a person deserves.

Both are important ways to make allowances, and are critical for loving others.

Are We Sweeping Dirt Under The Rug?

Making allowances does not mean approving of every negative behavior, but it does consider a few distinctions, because not all negative behaviors are the same. For clarification, it can be helpful to think in terms of three types:

—Some acts are not inherently wrong. They are simply quirks, idiosyncrasies, habits, or mannerisms we may find annoying. For these we make allowances.

—If the behaviors are clearly out of line by any reasonable person's assessment, we decide whether to make allowances or speak the truth in a loving way, keeping in mind what we learned in Chapter 7.

—Actions which cross legal or ethical boundaries must definitely be confronted, and perhaps reported to a professional who can help, if there could be grim consequences to the person or someone else.

Forgiveness (It's Beyond The Scope Of This Book)

Any discussion about making allowances can quickly become a dive into the waters of forgiveness. Forgiveness is wonderful. It's also enormously complex, running the continuum from the spilled glass of milk to devastating betrayals.

Most of us will need to forgive someone during our lifetime. But the terribly thorny, knotty world of forgiveness is beyond the scope of this book. This book deals with everyday relational interactions, where making allowances will cover the majority of what comes our way. It does not address complicated and unfathomable hurts and how to survive them.

For anyone who has faced serious issues and wrestles with questions of forgiveness and unforgiveness, it may be wise to meet with a spiritual mentor or professional therapist.

— — — — — — — — —

Chapter Summary

Loving others in ways they find meaningful will often require that we make allowances for certain behaviors. People's quirks may get under our skin, but this is no reason to be unloving.

Making allowances requires empathy. One relevant concept is the hot-cold empathy gap, which says that what people who are not currently in a particular situation think they would do in that situation can be much different from what they actually do when they're in that situation.

The hot-cold empathy gap states that there is no way to know what someone was going through in the moment of decision with all its pressures and influences. We can't even know how we ourselves would have acted in that situation if faced with the same factors. For these reasons, we should lighten up and make allowances.

Everyone is imperfect, including ourselves.

Many behaviors we find hard to accept are directly related to people's pasts and stories. Realizing this can make us more understanding.

People have weaknesses which affect how they act. We show love by cutting slack for them in those areas.

Mercy and grace are two critical elements in making allowances. Mercy means sparing someone from negative consequences. Grace involves acts of consideration that go beyond what a person deserves.

Making allowances does not mean sweeping blatant faults under the rug. When confrontation is needed, we find ways to do so lovingly.

Our commitment to loving our neighbor will be tested, because people have quirks, back stories and weaknesses. When it becomes difficult to show compassion, we now know the best response. It's simple but not always easy. Love makes allowances.

Have A Heart

Allowances. Mercy. Grace. Compassion. These are all admirable ways to treat people. The simplest phrase for encouraging someone along those lines might be to say "Have a heart." We can learn a few things about that from a famous fictional character.

The film version of *The Wizard Of Oz* is an adaptation of a book written by L. Frank Baum in 1900. Baum wrote 14 books about Oz. Number 12 tells the story of The Tinman.

Nick Chopper was a wood chopper. He and a girl named Nimmie Amee wanted to be married, but there was a problem: Nimmie was the personal servant of The Wicked Witch Of The East. The Witch did not want to lose her servant, so she put a spell on Nick Chopper's axe.

The spell caused the axe to cut off Nick's arm. He went to the tinsmith, where he received a new arm made of tin. The axe then cut off all Nick Chopper's other limbs, so the tinsmith fashioned replacements and even a neck to support Nick's head. Finally, the axe cut Nick's torso. The tinsmith made a new torso, but did not include within it a heart.

The Tin Woodman, as he was now called, was quite productive because he never got tired. Nimmie was thrilled with all the benefits of being engaged to a tin man, such as the fact that he could dance for hours.

Did The Tin Woodman marry Nimmie? No. He states, "I found that I no longer loved her. My tin body contained no heart, and without a heart no one can love."

People who seem to be without a heart sometimes accomplish much, but they miss out on the deepest experiences of life. With no heart we would escape pain, true, but we wouldn't feel joy either. And the saddest loss of all: we would not be able to love.

So always have a heart, and let it lead you to everything the life of love includes: showing empathy, extending mercy and grace, and making allowances for others. No doubt the Wizard Of Oz would agree.

9

Love Sets Boundaries

We need to have a talk on the subject of
what's yours and what's mine.
— Stieg Larsson, *The Girl With The Dragon Tattoo*

Take a plain sheet of paper and draw two non-overlapping circles on it, side by side. Beneath one circle, write the word "Me." Beneath the second circle, write "The Other Person."

You have just created a tool that could revolutionize your life. I use this diagram often. I call it "Circles Of Responsibility."

— — — — — — — — —

Free To Love

As you live according to the principles in this book, close relationships are likely to form. That's good. But if you begin to feel personally accountable for the outcomes of another person's decisions, accepting blame or credit, you've gone a step too far. Or if the interactions take on a caregiver and care-receiver dynamic, it's also time to make adjustments. In either case, some guidelines should kick in, so you can maintain proper boundaries, while still loving others.

You may have seen the person as an individual, listened to his or her story, asked questions, noticed the need, taken action, spoken the truth in love, and done your best to make allowances. But something went wrong. Maybe you feel burned out, because the person's needs seem never-ending. Perhaps he or she took offense at something you did or didn't do. Your intentions could be misunderstood. What now?

I suggest you review the Circles Of Responsibility diagram described above. Notice the circle marked "Me." Now ask yourself "Have I done everything I felt was my responsibility in this situation?" If so, that's all you can do. Your obligations are complete. Any response, or even a lack of response, belongs inside the other circle. And as you can see, that circle is marked "The Other Person," meaning it's not your responsibility.

This is freeing—freeing to all parties. Just as it liberates you from being accountable for someone else's responsibilities, it also liberates the other person from the obligation to act in any particular way, to appease you, or even to agree. His or her circle doesn't include or overlap your circle at all. You now have a wonderful freedom, the freedom to simply love.

Great Expectations?

We've got to be honest about our expectations. Are we hoping for specific results? Is there a certain way we want the other person to act? Do we feel owed something? Have we created in our minds an agenda or script for the relationship? Will we be disappointed if things don't work out as we've envisioned? If the answer to any of these questions is "Yes," we're on a dangerous path.

Ideally, the type of love explored in this book carries only the minimum of expectations, if any at all. But that's difficult. At times we may expect a certain response to something we've said or done. When that is the case, we have certain responsibilities.

First, be sure your expectation is realistic. If you've given someone a recipe for your grandmother's award-winning pasta sauce, it might not be reasonable to expect the person to tell you how delicious it was within a few days. He or she may have already had meals planned. Or just because you feel a certain book would speak to a friend in need doesn't mean the person will make time to read it or have the same positive reaction you did.

It's also up to you to make the person aware of your expectations, and to let that person decide whether he or she wants to agree to fulfilling them. This discussion should take place before you do whatever you're planning. Unmet expectations can harm a relationship. And expectations which are unexpressed will almost always go unmet, because the person obviously didn't know about them. Agreeing in advance resolves that.

Suppose you've noticed that someone who works in your office has a temporary need for transportation. She doesn't live far from you, so you take action by offering to carpool. You might even make an allowance by waiting 15 minutes at the end of your workday because she works later than you. Finally her car is repaired, and you're each back on your own.

A few months later, another colleague's car breaks down and is scheduled to be in the shop for more than a week. This person's house, however, is six miles out of your way. It seems only fair that he would offer to pay for gas. This is when you have to examine yourself to see if you have an expectation. If so, it is your responsibility to let your friend know. You might say "I'd be glad to give you a ride to and from work while your car's out of commission. I'll need to ask you to chip in for gas. Does that sound okay to you?"

I often spend significant time writing emails to people.

Occasionally, I don't receive a reply. If I find myself disappointed about that, it is because I was harboring an expectation which went unmet. But whose responsibility was that? Mine. Another person doesn't have an obligation to get back to me simply because I decide to write.

If there is a chance I will be upset by my email going unacknowledged, I can establish an agreement with the other person before I begin writing. I could contact him or her and say, "I have some thoughts I'd like to share by email. If that's okay with you, will you agree to let me know you received it and tell me what you think within a week?"

This works equally in reverse. There are times when someone will place unexpressed expectations on us. When those go unmet, because we were unaware of them, the person may become upset. It's possible at times like those for us to feel negatively toward ourselves, as though we failed. But that's unfair, because we are only responsible for efforts which belong squarely on our shoulders or to which we have agreed in advance.

Needy people sometimes feel entitled. If a person's car is broken down and yours is running fine, the person may imply, or outright state, that you are being unloving if you don't meet his or her transportation requests.

It's wise to clarify which efforts are your responsibility and the ones belonging to the other person. Then, by acting accordingly, both "Me" and "The Other Person" will have done our part in the Circles Of Responsibility. Any expectations should be reasonable and discussed in advance. If both parties agree that the expectations will be met, the situation can move on to the next step with everyone on board and content.

Responsible To vs. Responsible For

People have certain responsibilities to one another. Without this, society would be in chaos. Traffic would go down the same side of the street in both directions; stores would open and close arbitrarily. Basic order would be non-existent.

The same applies within personal relationships. There must be some reasonable set of responsibilities for them to function. But there is a huge difference between being responsible TO someone and being responsible FOR someone.

If I want to express love in practical ways, I'll honor my responsibilities TO the other person. I'll see that person as an individual, listen to his or her story, ask questions, keep confidences, notice the need, take action, speak the truth, and make allowances. I'll be true to my word, respect his or her opinions, and pay my fair share of mutual expenses. When I have a strong sense that something is amiss, I'll confront. These are a few of my responsibilities TO that person.

I am not, however, responsible FOR that person. What he or she does or doesn't do as a result of any input I offer is not my responsibility. I can't take credit if things go well, or blame myself or the other person if things go wrong. And I would not want to anyway. The only life I am responsible FOR is my own, and that is quite enough.

Parenting provides a clear example. When children are young, Mom and Dad do have responsibilities both to and for their sons and daughters. As those kids become adults, the "for" part of the equation drops off. Responsible parents will likely want to do anything they can to help their children no matter what their ages. But relationships between parents and grown children are healthiest when final decisions are left to those children alone.

Responsible to vs. responsible for is a key component in the art of setting boundaries as part of loving our neighbor.

Unknown Unknowns

Former Secretary of Defense Donald Rumsfeld is credited with stating that there are known knowns, known unknowns, and unknown unknowns. When it comes to the way another person should handle his or her life, we are operating largely in that last area: unknown unknowns.

Each of us has been given a human existence to manage. We call that "my life." For most of us, taking care of just one existence, our own, is plenty. And since we cannot know with certainty what is right for another person, beyond a few clear absolutes, it's best not to pretend otherwise.

Back to the Circles Of Responsibility diagram, the only life for which I am totally responsible is the one inside the circle labeled "Me." I can do my best to contribute in a loving way to people in the circle called "The Other Person." Ultimately, however, I must admit that when it comes to other people, the best direction for their lives are unknown unknowns to me. To use a more common version of what Rumsfeld said: regarding someone else's life, I don't even know what I don't know!

Again, this is liberating. Since I cannot possibly figure out the perfect direction for another person, I don't need to feel the weight of his or her choices. Likewise, that other person has no idea what is best for me, which leaves me free to move in directions I feel make good sense for myself, without outside pressure.

Although it's impossible for us to know the perfect direction for someone else, people often try. Here are a few humorous attempts that missed the mark:

—"Your work shows no creativity." This was said by the newspaper editor who fired Walt Disney.

—"He has minimal football knowledge and lacks motivation," stated a sportswriter describing Vince Lombardi, who later became head coach of the legendary Green Bay Packers, a dynasty in their time.

—"You are hopeless as a composer." – Beethoven's violin instructor.

—"It doesn't matter what he does, he will never amount to anything." That's what Albert Einstein's father heard from his son's school teacher.

Of course this does not negate the value of seeking counsel from wise mentors, literature, loving family members, and the like. We should be open to hearing from them and willing to consider their suggestions. In the final analysis, however, each person must make decisions for him or herself.

Unknown unknowns might be seen as a negative, but that's not necessarily the case. (Though in Donald Rumsfeld's world of global politics, they probably were.) If we accept them and stay in our own circle of responsibility, we'll create appropriate boundaries in relationships committed to love.

Who's Doing The Work?

Receiving love involves efforts on the other person's part as well. He or she will have to do some work for life to improve. This could involve revealing personal problems, sharing secrets which have been hidden for a long time, confessing faults, looking at painful places that are locked away, and a lot more. It takes mental or spiritual muscle to climb out of the pit. For these reasons, some people are afraid to let anyone get close. They are terrified of being loved and even push us away. Sadly, those men and women remain alone in their tough situations.

When two people are involved in a relationship where one is trying to help the other, the helper must make sure not to work harder than the one being helped.

If you reach out to someone multiple times in different ways with no response, perhaps the other person is not ready to receive the love you're offering. This doesn't make him or her deficient. It is simply one of those unknown unknowns. There comes a time when you have fulfilled everything in the "Me" circle in the diagram, and it's okay to put a hold on future efforts.

Financial bailouts and advice become a waste of resources if someone is spending foolishly and not making lifestyle changes. We can assume the person is doing what he or she feels is best, and not be judgmental. We can also decide we have done enough, and it's time to set a boundary where our assistance stops.

In most instances of one person assisting another, the person being helped must do the work for him or herself, while the helper acts solely as a guide. And I'll say it again: many people can benefit from the services of a trained therapist, counselor, life coach, business consultant, or other professional. A referral is sometimes the best course of action.

Making The Rare Exception

In rare cases we may feel a specific calling to make exceptions. Here is an example from personal experience.

A bad business investment can lead to all sorts of negative outcomes. So when a friend was close to putting his life savings on the line, I asked his permission to review the deal. My thirty-plus years of owning and operating a successful company might come in handy, I reasoned.

I soon found several factors he had not considered. When I presented the first few of these, each of which made the venture look questionable, my friend seemed uninterested in what I had to say, and undeterred from moving forward. At this point, my efforts could have stopped, as the final decision was clearly within his circle of responsibility, not mine.

For some reason, however, I continued to devote energy to the project. This was partially because I knew how serious the matter was, and that it would affect his life for years. But it was more than that; it was a sense of mission. I had no intention or desire to make the choice for him, but from deep within I felt a duty to be sure he had all the facts.

Over the next few days I contemplated many additional angles, building one financial model spreadsheet after another, and speaking with my friend regularly to show him the numbers, projections, and likely outcomes. I also raised non-financial concerns for him to ponder, such as the effects this endeavor could have on his time, stress level, marriage, and family life.

I was certainly working harder than he was, but it felt like the right thing to do. The verdict was still up to him, but my contribution did go above and beyond the usual input.

Though the point being made has nothing to do with the outcome of the situation, here's how it wrapped up: Once I exhausted my efforts, I asked my friend to sleep on it one more night. The next morning, he decided to pass on the deal. He later completed another transaction which netted a much better return with significantly less anxiety.

Because of an internal drive I cannot explain, this was one of those appropriate exceptions to the typical guideline of not working harder than the person you're trying to help.

That's Not My Job?

Setting boundaries and using the Circles Of Responsibility diagram does not reflect a "That's not my job" attitude. Instead, it's saying, "That IS my job," and "That other thing is your job." This is a much healthier, more realistic way of engaging with people than taking all the burden on ourselves.

We can't dictate other people's lives, for all the reasons stated here and more, so let's accept that and not pretend, or wear ourselves out in futile attempts. Instead, let's express love by taking on our own responsibilities, and only our own responsibilities, in relationships.

— — — — — — — — —

Chapter Summary

Do everything you can to express love to your neighbor. But be careful if you see yourself feeling responsible for the other person's decisions or reacting strongly to them. Also take note if the relationship morphs into one in which either party becomes more of a caregiver. Setting proper boundaries can keep these scenarios from getting out of control, or from happening in the first place.

The "Circles Of Responsibility" diagram is a helpful tool. It's two non-overlapping circles, labeled "Me" and "The Other Person." The circles represent each party's responsibilities.

Loving without expectations is a lofty aspiration, but not always possible. When expectations do exist, they must be reasonable and expressed in advance of any efforts being taken, so that an agreement can be made—or not—that the expectations will be met.

Each of us is responsible for one life, and only one life: our own. No one should presume to know the absolute best direction for someone else, beyond a few moral and legal absolutes.

We have certain responsibilities TO other people, but we are not responsible FOR them.

Don't work harder than the person you're trying to help, other than in rare cases where you feel a specific, strong sense of mission to do so.

Love sets boundaries. That's not uncaring; it's mature and appropriate. And it's part of loving your neighbor as yourself.

Boundaries Through The Centuries

The idea of setting boundaries in association with loving our neighbor has been around for at least a few hundred years.

In 1640, in the British publication *Outlandish Proverbs*, poet George Herbert was quoted as saying, "Love your neighbour, yet pull not downe your hedge." (That was about the same time the word "confront," meaning "the act of bringing two parties face to face," came to common usage. Hmmm.)

Apparently, the saying crossed the Atlantic Ocean and made it to America early on. Benjamin Franklin included similar wording in the *Poor Richard's Almanack* of April 1754. His version was, "Love thy neighbor; yet don't pull down your hedge."

This phrase, as is or with minor variations, has been quoted in countless essays, articles, lectures, and at least one play (*The Citizen*, by Arthur Murphy). It's even been memorialized through hundreds of memes across the internet.

The message seems to be universal. It's important to love our neighbor, and setting boundaries is an integral part of that. Without them, all kinds of difficulties can pop up. Leaving the hedge in place and healthy can help keep the relationship the same way.

10

Love Includes Yourself

I have found my hero, and he is me.
– Dr. George Sheehan

I remember the time I flew a few hours from home to attend a rather fancy function. Close to the airport, and with no time to spare, I got that sick feeling that fills every traveler with dread. I had forgotten to pack something. It was a necktie.

My first reactions were: anger at myself for being careless; sadness that I would likely have to waste money to buy a new tie, even though I have at least 40 of them at home I rarely wear; embarrassed because I would have to confess this absentmindedness to my wife, and a smattering of general negative self-talk.

Thoughts raced into my mind. "Do I really need a tie?" "Will everyone else be wearing a tie?" "What if I buy a tie and many of the men are not wearing ties? Then I'll be REALLY upset because I didn't have to buy one at all." "What if I don't buy a tie, and I'm the only man without one? That will be humiliating." "Maybe I can borrow a tie from another guy, but then he'll know that I messed up." The torment wouldn't stop.

I knew the mental battle might go on for a long time. It threatened to consume me and take the fun out of what was supposed to be an enjoyable trip.

Somehow, I was reminded of the importance of loving your neighbor as yourself. The "as yourself" part doesn't get a lot of attention, but I was fortunate enough to have reflected on this phrase a few days earlier. I realized it's not worth a whole lot to love someone as I love myself if I don't love myself.

So in my mind I asked a question "What would I do if my wife, one of our children or ANY 'neighbor' were in this exact predicament?" The answer was "I'd say 'No big deal, these things happen. You had a lot on your mind when packing. Let's buy you a [whatever] the first chance we get, so we won't have to think about this anymore.'" Then I'd go with that person while he or she purchased a replacement for the forgotten item (or likely get out my wallet if it were one of the kids), and put the whole situation out of my mind.

The obvious next question from me to me was "Can I love myself as I would love that neighbor?"

In the gift shop at the airport was a tie rack. I walked over to it, bought a necktie, and put it in my carry-on bag. Done. Peace.

I really like that tie now; not because it's so exquisite, but because of what it represents. It was an act of love to myself, perhaps paving the way for me to do a better job of loving my neighbor.

— — — — — — — — —

How Do I Love Thee, Me?

It's not very helpful to love our neighbor the way we love ourselves if we don't do a good job of loving ourselves.

Love ourselves? It sounds conceited and narcissistic. Not so, however. Conceited people live in deception. Their opinions of themselves are lofty beyond reality. And narcissists have to pretend they're better than everyone else in order to feel good about themselves. (These are gross simplifications, but the main nuggets are here.)

The self-love in loving our neighbor as ourselves does not include either of those distortions. It won't inflate reality or make comparisons with others. Instead, it brings out the best in us. It is self-acceptance, self-compassion, self-liking, and more.

One way to discover how well we love ourselves is to look at the very topics covered in this book. Can we apply those same practical expressions of love to the person in the mirror? Let's see.

There's Only One You

Love sees people as individuals. That goes for the way you see yourself as well. There is no one else like me; there is no one else like you. And before we make a joke by saying "Thank goodness," let's consider how remarkable this is.

You are [your name], the son or daughter of [parents' names], perhaps a sibling of [sibling(s) name(s) if applicable]. You may be a spouse and/or a parent, and maybe a grandparent or grandchild. You have a particular education, or are working in that direction. You were born in [insert location] on [date], and have since lived in [number] other places including [various cities, if applicable]. You spend your free time doing specific activities that appeal to you. These are your interests and hobbies. You like a certain type of book, a genre—or more than one—of movies, a style or styles of music. Maybe you listen to podcasts, and if so, you have a preferred playlist. You drive a certain make and model of car or truck, or rely on public transportation. You have a past that is exclusive to you, and goals for the future which are yours alone. There are joyous situations in your life, and problems keeping you awake nights. You even have a favorite ice cream. And on and on.

Did you notice? We didn't mention your career at all. Career is a big part of your life, of course, and an important piece of the overall you. But despite what society often implies, you are much more than your occupation, even if you love what you do, and feel called to serve society in that way. Still, that is only one part of who you are.

When all those factors are combined, and there are many others, it is easy to see your uniqueness out of the billions of people on the planet.

Everybody has a story. Think about yours. I'd bet the journey that brought you where you are today is fascinating. If it were made into a movie, people would laugh, cry, sit in suspense, cheer, and gasp at different parts of the show.

There are insights and observations which only you can make. There are contributions to the human race that no one other than you can provide, because they're based on experiences singular to you. This is true whether the road you traveled was covered in rose petals or filled with thorns.

Are you getting a sense of your individuality?

You're fortunate to be you. You are pretty amazing. It might be fun to get to know that person you call "Me" in a relational way instead of just having transactions with yourself which focus only on what you can achieve.

At some level you realize all this. It's hard to admit, though, because we have been subtly, or not subtly, trained that loving ourselves is bad. This book proclaims otherwise. Not only is loving yourself a good thing, it is essential if you're going to love others, since the goal is to love your neighbor as yourself.

A first step is to see yourself as an individual.

What Are You Saying? What Do You Hear?

When you speak to yourself, what do you hear? Is it loving, or not so much? Take a minute and listen. Many of us would never say to others the unkind things we tell ourselves. Here is some of my own past self-talk:

—During a morning run: "You are such a sluggish runner."
—Playing chess: "You've lost your edge."
—Getting a haircut: "Look at all that gray hair on the floor. You're so old."

While it could be worse, statements like that are not at all helpful.

There are a few ways to get in touch with our inner dialogue:

—The first is simply being aware of what is banging around in our heads. There's constant banter up there. What is it saying? Keep your internal ears open.
—The second method is similar but involves being more intentional. Find a quiet place to just sit and think. A memorable phrase for this is, "Pay attention to what has your attention."
—Alternatively, writing in a journal can help us articulate, and even discover, what's going on inside. A simple notebook works fine and digital options exist as well.

These techniques take deliberate effort, but they will help us gain clarity and unravel the complexities of our lives. If we work at it, we will hear ourselves into existence.

We must also listen for, find, and connect with our own emotions. We need to dive into our vocabulary and get to the root, rather than calling our feelings only "good" or "bad." Then we will be more apt to show empathy to ourselves.

Being aware of what we are telling ourselves, and the accompanying feelings, is a good start, but there is more work to be done. Remember, just because you have a thought or feeling does not make it so. Sometimes we have to push back against that negativity. That's where asking questions of ourselves becomes important. We might conduct an inner dialogue declaring that certain self-talk is not true, or that alternate truths exist which mitigate the sting.

I may not be as fast a runner as others, but if I dig a little, I discover the truth that I am out of bed and on the streets several days a week. Perhaps I should celebrate good health and discipline, rather than bemoaning my lack of speed. Grandmaster strengths are not required to enjoy chess. And gray hair? Well, it might be better than some alternatives!

Don't dwell on past mistakes. There is nothing to be gained by beating yourself up over them. You wouldn't do that to someone you love; it's just as damaging to do it to yourself. Every part of your story has contributed to who you have become. That's good news. Embrace it.

Love listens and asks questions. So listen to yourself, ask and answer some questions of yourself, and make sure what you hear expresses love.

You're Allowed To Have Needs Too

People who focus on loving others often bury their own needs as if they don't exist. They say "I'm well" and "Everything's fine," with superficial smiles and lives that are falling apart. Sound familiar? I hope not.

They continue purchasing on credit rather than seeking financial counsel, put off the doctor appointment while the symptoms worsen, know the relationship with the significant other is deteriorating, but avoid the conversation.

There is one person in your life who should love you enough to notice your need: You! Take advantage of that person for all he or she is worth.

Think about what's missing in your own life. Where are the gaps? What would you like to change? How could you feel more fulfilled? Have there been any victories lately? Do you need to congratulate yourself or celebrate?

Noticing is a conscious discipline. It requires initial efforts and ongoing practice. And love does that. It notices the need. So let's be serious about noticing the needs of ourselves.

Action!

Once we have noticed our own needs, we can take action to meet them.

If you're fortunate enough to be in a close relationship with someone who is good at loving others, you will benefit immensely by sharing your joys as well as the not so fantastic stuff with that person regularly. You might say "I received some exciting news today. Can I tell you about it?" or "I'm worried, and I have to talk to someone, or I am going to lose my mind. Can we get together?" (Sadly, those people are rare. You may not know anyone like that right now.)

The actions we take to show love to ourselves don't have to be monumental. Small efforts make a big difference. Don't feel like cooking? An expensive steak and lobster dinner is not required. Take-out grilled chicken from a favorite local diner can meet the need just as well. Feeling burned out? A week at a resort would be nice, but the luxury of watching a movie, even though other tasks are pressing, could do the trick. Treating yourself in ways like these will remind you you're loved … by you.

What do you do well? You probably find that enjoyable. So invest more time there. The realignment could be minor or life changing. Either way, if the result is the sense that you are loved, it will be worth it.

Do you know people who can make your life easier by taking care of tasks or projects you find difficult? Reach out. You would surely make an introduction if it could help someone else. That's a good enough reason to do it for yourself.

As we explored earlier, according to best-selling author Dr. Gary Chapman, each of us has a specific "love language"—one of five different ways in which we are most likely to feel loved. What's yours?

You might speak affirming words to yourself. Present yourself with a small gift. Do something nice for yourself, or let someone else serve you without feeling guilty about it. Spend quality time with yourself. Give out a few hugs. Choose one or more of those five options that you find most meaningful and proceed accordingly.

No doubt you have acquired a figurative tool shed full of techniques and methods for helping others. Those tools can benefit you as well. Remind yourself of a favorite motivational quote when you're feeling run down. Listen to a song which touches your soul. Read an article filled with pointers to help you deal with a personal situation. You worked hard pulling your life tools together. Be sure to take advantage of them.

People can be thought of as individuals who carry cups in need of being filled with practical love. They look to you as someone with a pitcher from which they can draw. But how do you fill your pitcher? Think about that. Then take some actions to show love to yourself.

Let's Look At The Truth

We've got to be truthful with ourselves, and we have got to express that truth in a loving manner. "Speaking the truth in love," applies to ourselves just as much as to others.

Confrontation means bringing parties face to face. An honest face to face (so to speak) with ourselves every so often is a good idea, and should be nothing to fear. It's all right to admit shortcomings, and even mistakes, but don't go overboard on the negatives. Instead, make a rational assessment and identify adjustments to help yourself improve, doing so with the love you deserve.

Ask yourself a few questions first. Are you angry with yourself for some reason? Punishing or blaming yourself for a decision that didn't turn out well? Have you made unfair value judgments about your motives? Could you be jumping to inaccurate conclusions? If so, you are violating the guidelines of effective confronting, and that can lead to a self-evaluation which is untruthful and unloving.

Feeling stuck in a bad situation can drain our hope and make us feel defeated. So if you hear words like "never" and "always" when you talk to yourself, challenge them. Or take a totally different approach and use some especially endearing words.

In 1935, a vocalist named Fats Waller released a song written by Fred Ahlert and Joe Young. That song has since been recorded by a long list of artists including Frank Sinatra, Nat King Cole, Barry Manilow, Dean Martin, Anne Murray, Willie Nelson, Bill Haley & His Comets, and even Paul McCartney. There must be something special about this piece of music for it to receive so much attention.

The song is called "I'm Gonna Sit Right Down and Write Myself a Letter."[1] As the title says, it tells the story of a person who plans to compose some mail to himself. He'll send it and pretend it came from a woman he loves.

This very special letter, according to the song, is going to contain words which are especially sweet. The writer will ask how the man is doing, wish him well, and sign off by saying, "with love," followed by symbols that depict kisses.

Just about anyone would like to find that in the mailbox. Why not express something similar from yourself to you?

Whether facing faults or delivering kudos, the truth needs to be spoken, and in a loving manner. That goes for speaking with yourself as well.

Bridging Our Gaps

When I was a teenager, I owned a used Chevy that got me to school and to a part-time job. One day I decided to drive up to the Honda motorcycle dealership, just to look. I had no intention of buying. A car AND a motorcycle were out of the budget, and two wheels as my only form of transportation would be crazy. I'd only be observing—no doubt about it.

But then there it was. The most beautiful machine I had ever seen. A Honda SL350. Burnt orange in color. Thirty-three incredible horsepower and a top speed of 86 miles per hour. What's more, the salesman was a really likeable guy, and this business took cars in trade. Oh happy day! I rode that baby home.

Before long, however, reality set in. Even in Florida where it's usually warm, a motorcycle is not practical 100% of the time. There are rainy days, packages to carry, and events that involve giving a ride to friends. Things between the bike and me didn't work out, so just a few months later I sold it at a significant loss and went back to a beat-up car. This time a Ford.

It was a perfect example of the hot-cold empathy gap. Reminder: What we do in a situation (called the hot state) is often much different from what we envisioned we would do in that situation as we thought about it before or after it occurred (the cold state). This is known as the Hot-Cold Empathy Gap.

In my cold state, prior to setting foot inside that Honda showroom, I was certain I would not be making a purchase. Then in the hot state of falling in love with a motorcycle, and imagining how much fun it would be to have the wind in my face, plus being under the influence of sales techniques, I did something much different from what I had predicted. Later, back in a cold state, I couldn't believe the foolishness of my decision.

The hot-cold empathy gap is a reality. Understanding this, we need to cut ourselves some slack. When we're in an after-the-fact cold state, it's harmful to look back and kick ourselves for acting less admirably than we wish we had during the hot state. Instead, realizing there were many factors pressing us which felt powerful at the time, even though later they seemed obviously unwise, is an act of loving ourselves.

Let's bridge the gap of our own actions with empathy.

Making Allowances

There are a few quirky things about this person I call "Me." I annoy myself now and then. This could be a problem, since I'm pretty much stuck with me. So if I'm serious about loving myself, I've got to make allowances.

The same goes for you.

Factors from the past or present may be catalysts for

your idiosyncrasies. And of course you have blind spots and weaknesses like everyone. These are additional reasons to lighten up on yourself.

You're just as worthy of mercy and grace as anyone. So if you make an honest mistake, or don't achieve a goal, take a pass on at least some of the negative consequences you could self-inflict, and show mercy instead. And now and then give yourself grace by an act of consideration that goes beyond what you deserve.

Moral, ethical, or legal failures can't be ignored under the guise of making allowances. If you commit one of those, you'll have to face the cause, the behavior, and the outcomes head on. Should you find yourself dealing with what feels like the impossibility of forgiving yourself, or some other serious issue, give yourself permission to speak with a professional therapist.

We've all got quirks—even you. But love makes allowances. Accept yourself as you are and make allowances for yourself.

That's Far Enough

There's only so much you can do. Time can't be expanded. Money is finite. Your talents are what they are. Can you accept these limitations and be at peace within their boundaries? Can you be realistic about your goals? You'll have to in order to truly love yourself.

Keep your expectations of yourself in check. If you need eight hours sleep to function coherently, don't expect to be fresh after staying up until 2:00 a.m. If handyman projects aren't your thing, don't pressure yourself by volunteering to install your neighbor's new sink. It's best not to set expectations which put you in a predicament and create stress for yourself.

These may sound like boundaries between you and another person, but they are actually internal. They reflect what you're asking of yourself, not what someone else is asking of you. Make your life a little easier by remembering that love sets boundaries, including the boundaries you set for yourself.

— — — — — — — — — —

Chapter Summary

We can't love our neighbor unless we love ourselves. We express self-love in the same practical ways we show love toward others.

We see ourselves as individuals with unique stories. We listen to ourselves, ask ourselves questions, notice our own needs, and take action to meet them. As we engage in self-talk, we do it with truth and in a loving manner. We show empathy toward ourselves, and because we recognize our own idiosyncrasies, we make allowances for them. And we set boundaries, being careful not to put excessive demands or set unrealistic expectations on that person known as "me."

If we're feeling overly pressured, overwhelmed by the demands of loving others, or guilty for taking reasonable care of ourselves, we are likely out of balance. It's time to work on mastering this important aspect of practical love: love includes yourself.

Crew Member Instructions

There is a ritual that occurs on every commercial flight on every airline in the country. Before takeoff, the flight attendants go through a speech, during which a few passengers pretend to be interested while others don't pay attention at all. There is something in those crew member instructions which provides a lesson in loving ourselves.

One thing the flight attendants say is similar to this: "Should we experience a loss in cabin pressure, oxygen masks will drop down from the ceiling compartment located above your head." After explaining how to use them, the flight attendant will add, "Please secure your own mask before assisting those around you."

Getting your own oxygen mask on before attempting to help someone else is wise. How much can you benefit another person if you yourself are gasping for air?

Likewise, if we neglect our own need for love, we will have little capacity to express love to someone else. For us to love others, it's important to first love ourselves.

I can't pay for a friend's lunch when my credit cards are at their limits. I've got to get my own financial affairs in order first, then I will be able to help others. It's hard to see my neighbor as an individual when I'm feeling like an insignificant drop in the sea of humanity. Or to be a compassionate listener when dealing with piles of unprocessed issues of my own.

This need not be taken to extremes. We don't have to be perfect before we can reach out. But we have got to make sure we are working on addressing our own needs. With those bases covered, we can give attention to helping others. And that makes for a much smoother flight.

PART THREE

Living The Life Of Practical Love

11

Words Of Warning / Words Of Encouragement

The course of true love never did run smooth.
– William Shakespeare

A friend of mine who's a professional therapist says this: "If you're going to love others, prepare to have your heart broken." That's good advice.

Loving your neighbor as you love yourself is hard work. Challenges arise on two distinct levels. First, there are practical skills to be learned, which we have been discussing. And then there are the more abstract concerns which are the subject of this chapter.

As you will see, these concerns involve some downsides you're likely to encounter. But the upside is terrific, so any difficulties that come with this life are certainly worth enduring.

– – – – – – – – – –

What's Obvious To You Isn't Obvious To Them

Having read this far, you have a new problem. You know too much now.

You understand that everyone is an individual with a story. So when you notice people treated as mere objects, caught in transactional rather than relational interactions, you find it emotionally painful.

When you overhear conversations in which each party is talking only about him or herself, without asking even a single question, you hurt inside.

It saddens you to observe people being treated harshly because of their minor quirks which could easily be overlooked by making allowances.

Wherever you go, you're bound to witness unloving activities. The loving alternatives will be obvious to you but not necessarily obvious to others, which might be tough for you to bear.

Anybody There?

Another occupational hazard of this life is loneliness.

You will have plenty of incoming contacts, but a large percentage will be requests for your listening ear. It's not always that people are insensitive, it is just that they themselves feel isolated and overwhelmed with their own needs. Plus, they have never been taught what it looks like to show love in practical ways.

Still, true friendships are possible. If you have one (or more) right now, and I hope you do, value that person as a precious gift. He or she may be lonely too. So make an alliance to show love to each other, and you will both feel a lot better. As for those with whom you are not as close, perhaps you can cultivate their tendencies to show love, helping them grow.

Don't succumb to loneliness. Find a few people who care and reach out.

Parkinson's Law Applied To Love

There is a business principle called Parkinson's Law which states, "Work expands to fill the time available for its completion." The word "work" could be replaced by the words "showing love" and the saying would be equally true: "Showing love expands to fill the time available for its completion." And by the way, showing love is never complete.

If you set out to love others as you love yourself, you could become inundated with those who want to get on your calendar. You can't blame them. Chances are that few people relate to them the way you do.

Loving others can be as demanding as an additional part-time job. But don't forget that you control the schedule, and it is perfectly appropriate to set healthy boundaries.

So Many Concerns

As you learn of people's financial problems, marital difficulties, rebellious children, health issues, and more, it can easily affect your own sleep. It is nearly impossible not to carry their concerns within yourself. After all, you care.

Remember the Circles Of Responsibility diagram? It applies here as well. By showing love in practical ways you will have significant positive effects on people. Still, there is only so much you can do, and only so many for whom you can do it. Situations beyond your capabilities do not belong in the circle labeled "Me." To free yourself from becoming overwhelmed, you will have to make peace with that truth.

And More

Somebody said, "No good deed goes unpunished." While I don't live by negative sayings, this one is sometimes fitting. Your efforts may be criticized for not being enough, judged as insincere, not appreciated, or not even acknowledged.

Then there's the problem of misunderstood intentions. When people draw conclusions that are far from accurate, the emotional pain can be horrible. Sadly, resolution is not always achieved no matter how well you try to explain.

There are definitely a few potholes on the road of loving your neighbor.

On The Other Hand, It's Glorious

The life of loving your neighbor as yourself has tremendous upsides for everyone involved. Let's consider a few ways that your own life is enhanced when you display practical love to others:

—Seeing people as individuals and hearing their stories provides the most fascinating front row seat on Earth.

—Learning to be relational, rather than transactional, adds a dimension of lightheartedness and fun to human interactions. It makes every conversation more enjoyable.

—When you listen and ask questions, give your full attention, and connect with people's feelings, you hear them into existence—such a wonderful gift to the person, and an honor for you. Plus, you become an expert at discerning the subtleties of a full range of emotions, which gives you another valuable life skill.

—Hearing others' secrets is a privilege; it means you have earned a special place of trust in their lives. And being trusted is a great feeling.

—Everyone has needs. By noticing those needs and taking action to meet them, you will know you have eased people's suffering and increased their joy, which in turn increases your own joy.

—Learning to set and express reasonable expectations, mastering the art of confrontation, grasping concepts such as reticular formation and the hot-cold empathy gap, taking steps to make allowances for others despite their flaws and idiosyncrasies— these aspects of personal development will benefit many areas of your life, from business to marriage.

—When you show mercy and grace, you take part in the currency of saints and deity. The standards you use to measure others will become the ones used to measure you. That's good news, because we all need mercy and grace now and then.

—The (metaphorical) tools in your shed, which you access to benefit others, will come in handy for yourself as well.

—Understanding the importance of setting boundaries, and of loving yourself will free you to take care of the person you call "Me," without reservation or feelings of guilt.

— — — — — — — — — —

In all these ways and more, showing practical love to your neighbor can increase your ability to love yourself. Likewise, loving yourself can further energize you to love others. It's a cycle that builds both areas, making you a better person at the same time as it helps someone else.

The importance of practical love, and the effect it could have on all mankind, are valid reasons to study and practice its principles, just as you have been doing. Then, when each evening comes to a close, and your mind quiets down for the day, you'll feel satisfaction that cannot be gained from any other pursuit, as you realize you are fulfilling your highest and best use in relation to other humans.

This life is just plain glorious after all.

12

A Case Study – Fictional, but based on true accounts

*If you find it in your heart
to care for somebody else,
you will have succeeded.*
– Maya Angelou

Her name is Elisabeth, but everybody calls her Lis. "Like Liz, but with an s instead of a z," she tells them. She has no clue why her parents saddled her with that spelling. They were free spirits after all. Something about a former queen of Hungary, they said.

Lis spends her days sitting behind the reception desk at a CPA firm, two nights most weeks doing Pilates, and random hours with one or more of the close-knit group of girls who call themselves the Pitt Crew after their shared crush on Brad Pitt. The rest of her time goes to reading classic literature with her housemate, a cat named Geronimo. And recently a significant other relationship has gotten more serious. It's not a bad life for a 34-year old.

You would never suspect that Lis has skills which can literally change the world. Or at least the world of a fair number of people with whom she comes in contact. You see, Lis takes seriously the idea of loving her neighbor in practical ways, and loving herself, too. She's learned what that means, and she puts her knowledge to work every day. Let's peek inside Lis' life.

– – – – – – – – – –

Lis and Valerie met on Valerie's first night at the Pilates studio. They were each drinking from their water bottles after the session. "Hydrating," as the fitness crowd calls it.

The conversation got rolling when Lis caught Valerie's eye. "Wow, she was tough on us tonight," Lis said, nodding toward the instructor.

"Well it sure felt hard to me," Valerie replied. "I'm new to all this. Trying to get back in shape. I used to work out all the time, but I had to back off for a while."

A thought crossed Lis' mind that there might be a story behind that remark.

"Hi, I'm Lis."

"Valerie. Or Val. Doesn't matter."

"You did great, Val. I was struggling too hard to notice much, but from what I did see you're a natural. What kind of workouts were you doing in the past?"

"A lot of cardio. Elliptical, stair stepper, treadmill. That type of thing."

"That can be grueling. What gym did you go to?"

"Downtown Health Club," came Valerie's answer. "But there was this guy there. It was good for a while, then it went south."

"A guy. That'll do it," Lis chuckled. "I'm all ears if you ever want to talk. Are you doing okay now?"

"Pretty much. And I might take you up on that. But I've got to go. I turn into a pumpkin promptly at 9:00 p.m. Nice talking with you."

"Nice talking with you too, Val."

Over the next few weeks, the two saw each other nearly every Tuesday and Thursday nights. They'd chat for a few minutes after the workout, but Val always had to leave right away. They also exchanged cell phone numbers. One day a text message showed up on Lis' screen.

"Hi. It's Valerie. Any chance of meeting at the smoothie bar a half hour before class tonight?"

All Lis had to do was type the word "See," and because she'd sent the message so many times, her phone auto-filled the rest: "you there then."

The thumbs up emoji came back.

Lis arrived at the smoothie shop right on time. After waiting a few minutes, she decided to order. "Medium strawberry mango with low fat yogurt and a flax seed boost," she said to the twenty-something young man at the counter. "And how are you doing today? Your name's Andrew, right?" she added, noticing his name badge.

"Andrew. Yeah. I'm fair I guess."

"Fair you guess. That almost sounds a little sad. What's going on?" asked Lis as she handed him her credit card.

"I've been up since 5:15, and I'm worn out," Andrew answered.

"Wow. That's early," was Lis' response. Truth be told, Lis was jarred awake at 5:00 a.m. that morning when the neighbor's dog wouldn't stop barking. "I'm feeling kind of tired myself," she said, without going into detail. "What gets you up at such a crazy hour?"

"School. We have finals next week."

"Finals, that's rough. What are you studying?"

"Computer science."

Lis glanced behind her to make sure there wasn't a line. "Very good. It's a broad field. Any particular area?"

"I want to get into cyber security."

Just then, Valerie walked in. Lis quickly waved, then turned back to Andrew. "There's a vast need there. You'll probably have plenty of job offers once you get your degree."

Val greeted Lis, then told Andrew the drink she wanted. A group of four college guys approached the counter, so Val and Lis stepped aside. Minutes later their smoothies were up, and they sat at one of the wooden contoured booths.

—————————

The small talk was out of the way quickly. Lis noticed a look of worry come across her friend's face. "You mind if I tell you something personal?" Valerie asked.

"Not at all. Please do."

"It's pretty raw."

"That's all right. I can handle it," Lis assured her.

"So, remember when I told you there was this guy at the gym where I used to go?"

Lis nodded.

"And remember when I said things didn't turn out well with him?"

"Of course."

Valerie took a sip of her smoothie. "And you've noticed that I'm always in a hurry to get home after Pilates?"

"Sure, Val, but I didn't want to pry."

"That's because I'm on probation, and I have to call in

from my land line every night at nine and leave a message in their system. The guy, he and I started dating. He was into oxy. We were out, and he ran a stop sign. Got pulled over. We had pills in the car. It was horrible. I spent exactly forty-six and a half hours in jail before I could post bond. My parents spent a ton on the best lawyer we could find. A miracle worker. He made a deal. Time served, four weeks house arrest, and 20 months' probation. The guy's serving five years. I hope I never see him again. Now I have a record, and I can't be out past nine for another year and a half."

Lis recognized this was serious news—even shocking. She hadn't suspected any of it. Inside, her thoughts were racing. She knew, however, that she needed to maintain a calm exterior so her friend would be comfortable enough to keep talking if she wanted to without feeling judged.

"What a heavy burden, Val," Lis said. "Is this why you wanted to get together, or is there more?"

"Unfortunately, there's more. I missed my call last night. Only by about six minutes, but still. I think I could get picked up and taken back to jail any time. It's bad."

Lis could hear the fear in Valerie's voice and see it in her eyes. "That sounds terrifying. I can understand why you're upset. Your brain must be playing all kinds of scary tricks on you."

The two talked a little longer. It was clear to Lis that this situation wasn't going away any time soon, so she made a suggestion. "Let's skip Pilates tonight. I'll go home and feed Geronimo, then stop at the grocery store. My specialty is tacos. We can eat comfort food until you call in at nine. If there's a problem, maybe the system will alert you."

Lis continued. "I can spend the night if you want, and we'll call your attorney in the morning. He should be able to tell you if there's anything going on. I probably can't do much, but

I'll be there for moral support."

They agreed, and left the smoothie bar, taking their unfinished drinks with them. Before she went out the door, Lis walked up to the cash register. "I hope you ace your finals, Andrew," she said. He looked surprised, smiled, and replied, "Thanks."

— — — — — — — — — —

Lis showed up at Val's place as they'd planned. Dinner was just what they needed, and the 9:00 p.m. call was nothing out of the ordinary. Lis fell asleep on the sofa during the first recorded episode of *Grey's Anatomy*.

The next morning, Valerie's attorney was able to determine there was no violation of probation warrant out for her. After a while Val stopped worrying, and her life returned to what had become normal.

Val and Lis met for smoothies before Pilates at least once a week. This gave them an extra hour or so to talk. At least theoretically. It was usually closer to 45 minutes once Valerie arrived. Not one to waste time, Lis always brought a book to read while she waited.

On one of those evenings, a male voice interrupted their conversation. "Val. Hey, great to see you."

"Good to see you too, Ryan," she replied. "This is my friend Lis. Ryan works with me. Three cubicles down."

"Nice to meet you."

"Likewise."

As Ryan went to get his drink, Valerie excused herself to the ladies' room. Next thing Lis knew, Ryan was back at her booth, taking a seat where Val had been. It was only the two of them.

"I know we just met, but you obviously hang out with Val, and I've got a question," he said.

This seemed odd to Lis, but she had seen stranger things. "What is it?" she replied.

"Like Val told you, we work at the same place. She was out for a month not long ago and she never told anybody why. We're all concerned. Do you know anything?"

Warning lights flashed in Lis' head. "I can't really say," she answered.

"You sure?" Ryan asked. "She hasn't told you?"

Lis wasn't about to go there. "Maybe you could ask her."

"Maybe. Thanks anyway. Gotta go. Say 'Bye' to Val for me."

It wasn't long before Valerie returned to her seat. "Ryan's gone already?"

"Yeah. He was in a hurry. He told me to tell you 'Goodbye'."

"Fine with me," Val said. "I don't really like talking with him. Ryan's the office gossip. Anything he hears winds up all over the department. Where were we before he walked in? Oh right, I was just about to tell you about my mom."

"Great," Lis replied. "You can help me work through some feelings toward my mom as well. In fact we might have to skip class again and order some more smoothies. Moms are a big topic for sure."

They both laughed.

— — — — — — — — — —

There was something different about Valerie at one of the Pilates classes. Her attitude around Lis wasn't the same. Lis thought it might be her imagination, but when it happened the next time as well, Lis sent Val a text.

"Everything okay? It seems like something's bothering

you lately."

"Don't worry about it."

"Now I'm even more concerned, Val," Lis wrote. "Sounds like we ought to talk. Would that be all right with you?"

No reply.

Deafened by the silence, Lis knew it was time to take the conversation off the screen and into the realm of voice to voice, so she called Val's number. "I won't force you, but if you're willing, I think it would be good for us to talk," Lis said. "Are you up for that?"

Val agreed. They made arrangements to meet at a nearby park and go for a walk.

Waiting for Valerie, Lis wondered what this might be about. After some awkward small talk, Lis paused and caught Val's eye. "I sense there's something on your mind, Val. Our friendship means a lot to me, so let's get it resolved."

"I can't deny that I'm upset," Valerie replied, "but I really like you and I've never been good at this kind of thing. I don't want to get into a shouting match."

"It's not going to be that way," said Lis. "I don't believe in those kinds of confrontations. We don't have to lose our tempers. We can just talk."

Lis listened intently as Valerie told her she felt hurt and angry when Lis didn't come to her birthday party two weeks before. It seemed to Val that she wasn't important to Lis, and maybe their friendship was not as deep as she had thought.

Lis reflected a moment, then said, "Wow. I can see how much that hurt you. I had no idea, Val. I'm so sorry."

Val nodded, tearing up momentarily, then tried to brush it off by laughing. "It's okay. No big deal."

Lis stopped walking and turned to her friend. "Val, it is a big deal, and I'm so glad you told me." Lis explained that she'd seen something about a party on social media, but it looked like it was a small get together for family. "I honestly didn't know I was invited."

Lis paused. "Let's try to be upfront and ask each other directly for what we want. Like give each other a heads up when something is important to us. Then we can decide ahead of time if we can do it. Sound fair?"

"Yeah. I like that."

"Good. I'm relieved. Feel like a birthday smoothie, girlfriend?"

"If you're treating!"

— — — — — — — — —

Elisabeth and Valerie remain close to this day. Over the course of their relationship there have been all sorts of interactions.

Friendships go both ways, and without a doubt Val has been there for Lis on occasion. Like the day Lis got a call from a state trooper. Her brother Derek, coming home from working the late shift at the mall, had been T-boned by a drunk driver. Lis was frantic, and felt so comforted when Val showed up at the hospital and just hugged her while she cried. It took four hours of surgery and nine weeks of recovery for Derek's internal injuries, punctured lung, and broken ribs to heal.

Understandably, Lis took a break from Pilates and basically everything else. Val gave her some space during that time, which Lis appreciated.

The Pitt Crew came through for Lis big time during Derek's hospital stay. Casseroles a couple times a week so she wouldn't have to cook. Stopping by to take care of Geronimo on days when Lis went to visit Derek straight from work. And an understanding ear as Lis dealt with intense anger at the jerk who took the wheel of a car after drinking, bringing a trauma to her whole family and nearly killing her little brother.

At one point, Val started hanging out with a guy who gave Lis some concern. He just didn't seem upstanding, and Lis didn't want her friend to make a big mistake again. This called for another walk in the park.

Lis expressed her observations, gave Val a few things to think about, and left it there. Val did take Lis' input seriously, ultimately ending it with the guy a few weeks later. It wasn't a surprise when they saw a report that he'd been busted for passing bad checks. "I sure know how to pick 'em," Val texted one day. Lis was empathetic, realizing that there's no way she could predict what she herself would have done in a similar situation—being lonely and having a good-looking man give her attention. And Lis had to admit she'd made mistakes in that department herself.

Speaking of guys, Lis met someone nice: Keith, a massage therapist with his own sports injury practice. For a while when Keith first came on the scene, they were together all the time, so Lis barely saw Val for three months outside of Pilates. But that's how relationships are. They ebb and flow. Friends might connect intensely for years, then barely speak for a season. The good ones can pick up right where they left off.

Val's tendency of being late does bother Lis. But, Lis reasons, that isn't a moral or legal shortcoming, and keeping the bonds between them strong is more important than correcting everything that personally annoys her. After all, Lis understands that everyone, including herself, has quirks. Besides, who is she to tell another woman how to run her life? So Lis makes an allowance for this and doesn't mention it.

One morning a reminder popped up on Lis' calendar; Valerie's probation was ending in two weeks. Lis suggested Val take the day off work and scheduled a six-hour spa session for the two of them. Massage, manicure, pedicure, facial, and a farm-to-table organic lunch. Lis' treat. She even arranged for a limo to take them there and back. They still talk about it.

The calls, text messages, e-mails, and requests to meet up became a lot more frequent when Valerie's cousin took a job three states away and told Val there was an opening that would be perfect for her. Val was practically obsessing, thinking about whether to leave her current employer, move, ask her boss for more money, ditch it all and go back to school nights, or look for other options.

Lis repeatedly encouraged Val to consider the pros and cons, update her resume, get references on paper, try to arrange an interview, and all the rest. Lis also told Val a few quick highlights of how she'd come to apply at the CPA firm and the steps involved in getting hired there.

For some reason, Val wasn't following through, even though she wanted to talk about the position and every little detail surrounding it for hours, going over the same ground every time. Finally Lis realized she'd done everything she felt was her responsibility to Val and was working harder on the situation than Val was.

"I'm the one losing sleep and energy over this," Lis admitted to herself. So Lis told Val that she trusted her to make a good career decision on her own when she was ready. Lis added that she was going to back out of future discussions on the topic. Val didn't understand at first, but it worked out.

When Val finally did interview and accepted an offer, Lis coordinated a bunch of friends from her apartment complex to help Val load the rented truck and relocate. One guy even drove with her the entire way. He obviously had an interest in Val, and they wound up getting together. Lis isn't the manual labor type, so she made a huge batch of her famous tacos.

— — — — — — — — — —

What's amazing about Lis is that Val is only one of the many people her life touches. There are a handful of people in Lis' orbit who get her attention. Some she met at work, a few at a book club, and others just out and about.

Through the years Lis has picked up several tidbits of wisdom, techniques for dealing with different situations, books and articles, and more that seem to be helpful whenever she passes them along.

An elderly man happened to sit next to Lis in the waiting room at the veterinary office when she took Geronimo for his annual checkup. Lis and the man began talking. As it turned out, his wife needed a wheelchair, and they couldn't afford one. Lis notified her neighbor who's a social worker. They contacted the right service and hooked the woman up with a brand-new electric model.

Understandably, the lady was pleased with the device, but it seemed to Lis that there was something more than that going on. Sure enough, even the smallest gift, such as a candy bar or a card, was very meaningful to this woman. So through the convenience of online shopping, Lis is making a difference in an elderly person's life on a regular basis.

A chance meeting at the coin laundry when the washing machine in Lis' unit broke down turned into a conversation with Pam, a single mom. That encounter became an occasional Scrabble night. The game is secondary; Pam just likes spending time with people.

Andrew at the smoothie bar was a regular connection for a while. On one of her visits, Lis gave him a printout of an article she saw online: "Top 10 Careers In Cyber Security." He eventually graduated and pursued bigger things.

There was the young woman at an Administrative Assistant's training conference. During the buffet lunch Lis saw her take her food to a table away from the main dining area. When Lis finished eating, she poured herself an extra glass of iced tea, went over, and asked, "Would you like some company?"

"If you want to," the girl replied, which was enough for Lis to sit down. It came up that the girl was struggling with an issue so severe that dealing with it was way over Lis' head. Lis expressed her concern and referred the woman to a therapist.

It doesn't stop there, but you get the idea.

Now and then Lis feels overwhelmed with all the demands on her life. Listening to people's stories and hurts can get tiring. One friend from the Pitt Crew is Lis' sanctuary. They sit and talk about anything from Aristotle and Plato to Michael Kors and Gucci. And they laugh every time they're together. Lis and Keith enjoy each other too, of course. Lis takes herself off the grid now and then for both these special people—no phone, laptop, or tablet—though in a way she does it for herself. She also doesn't mind being alone, so if she feels the need, she rents a cabin in the mountains for a long weekend. Just her, Geronimo, and a Dickens novel.

Lis' heart has been broken a few times from investing herself in people when it didn't turn out as she had hoped, her intentions have been misunderstood, or the people she was helping wanted more than she could give. And she's had to turn the other way when someone wronged her, as well as give in to people when maybe it wasn't deserved. Then again, she's not perfect herself, and others no doubt have done the same for her.

It's a very enjoyable, fulfilling life this woman has; Lis with an s instead of a z, probably named after a former queen of Hungary, daughter of parents who were free spirits. She can't imagine devoting herself to a higher purpose than loving her neighbor. Which is not surprising, because aside from the mandate to love God, there is none.

13

Ready For Harvest

The mark of a true shepherd is this:
love for the sheep.
— JR StJohn

We end this exploration of the practical ways to express love by going back to where our study began: with a few more words from Jesus of Nazareth. On one occasion he said, "Look at the fields, for they are ready for harvest." Another time, he expressed something similar: "The harvest is abundant." What does all that mean?

These words come just after we're told that Jesus looked out upon the crowds who came to him in desperation, and he "felt compassion for them, because they were weary and worn out, like sheep without a shepherd." That is the context in which it was said "The fields are ready for harvest," and "The harvest is abundant."

Now it makes sense.

The part of this world we touch every day is a field filled with people who feel weary ... worn out ... like sheep in need of a loving shepherd. They crave to be seen as individuals. They want to tell their stories. They wish someone would notice their needs and take action to meet them. They could benefit by hearing truth spoken in love, by someone making allowances for them, and even by boundaries set for their benefit.

People are the harvest. Calling the need "abundant" is quite an understatement.

The premise of this book is that there is nothing more important on this planet, no higher or better use for a human, than to love God and to love our neighbor in practical ways. And we've got to love ourselves as well, or we'll burn out in the process.

The opportunities are limitless. Loving your neighbor is a calling in high demand, that will take all you are willing to give it.

Because the fields are ready for harvest, and the harvest is abundant.

— — — — — — — — —

And what you have heard from me ...
commit to faithful men [and women]
who will be able to teach others also.

Afterword

I first got the inspiration for this book around 2013. It marinated for a while, and then I gave a 20-minute talk on the subject in 2015. Four years later, in early 2019, I started writing, working on the manuscript nearly every day for well over a year before it was published.

It's said that a book is never complete—it is simply abandoned. That is certainly true in my experience writing *Loving Your Neighbor: A practical guide*. Several times after I thought I was finished, another facet of the life of showing love has entered my space. World events create new needs, technology presents more ways to interact, the flow of society introduces problems—and their corresponding opportunities—which we could not have imagined previously. And every relationship we develop, each with a unique story, adds a dimension to our understanding and experience.

Hopefully, some people will resonate with what's written, because they are living this life already. Others may discover a few new ideas and turn them into new behaviors. And for every endeavor there are critics. But since neither I nor what I have written are perfect, any thoughts about this topic are valuable. They only make the message better.

So I present to you a book unfinished. Perhaps that's good. Because you, the reader, can now complete it in ways which are revealed to you alone. I encourage you to embrace that challenge through your journey in this greatest of all human-to-human pursuits: loving your neighbor.

Steve Fales

Notes

Chapter 3: Love Sees People As Individuals
1. "World Population Clock: 7.7 Billion People – Worldometers," accessed July 17, 2020, https://www.worldometers.info/world-population/, Further citations of this work are given in the text.

Chapter 5: Love Notices The Need
1. "Wikipedia: Kevin Hines," Wikimedia Foundation, last modified June 12, 2020, https://en.wikipedia.org/wiki/Kevin_Hines.

2. Chelsea Robinson, "Bellevue Teacher Moved to Tears by Students Pooling Money to Replace His Stolen Shoes," January 30, 2020, https://www.ketv.com/article/bellevue-teacher-moved-to-tears-by-students-pooling-money-to-replace-his-stolen-shoes/30714218.

3. John Madden, "Bellevue Teacher Moved to Tears After Students Replace Stolen Sneakers," January 30, 2020, https://www.youtube.com/watch?v=UKg0QbwEm_Y.

4. Bruce Goldman, "New Imaging Method Developed at Stanford Reveals Stunning Details of Brain Connections," Stanford Medicine: News Center, November 17, 2010, https://med.stanford.edu/news/all-news/2010/11/new-imaging-method-developed-at-stanford-reveals-stunning-details-of-brain-connections.html.

5. Christopher Chabris, and Daniel Simons, "The Invisible Gorilla: And Other Ways Our Intuitions Deceive Us," Theinvisiblegorilla.com, 2010, http://www.theinvisiblegorilla.com/gorilla_experiment.html.

6. J.D. French, "Scientific American," Volume 196: Issue 5, May 1957, https://www.scientificamerican.com/magazine/sa/1957/05-01/.

7. Yogi Berra and Dave Kaplan, *You Can Observe A Lot By Watching: What I've Learned about Teamwork from the Yankees and Life* (Hoboken, NJ: Wiley, 2009).

Chapter 6: Love Takes Action
1. "Facts about Mother Teresa," accessed July 17, 2020, https://www.biographyonline.net/facts-about-mother-teresa/.

Chapter 7: Love Speaks The Truth
1. "Online Etymology Dictionary," accessed July 17, 2020, https://www.etymonline.com/.

Chapter 10: Love Includes Yourself
1. "Wikipedia: I'm Gonna Sit Right Down and Write Myself a Letter," Wikimedia Foundation, last modified June 1, 2020, https://en.wikipedia.org/wiki/I'm_Gonna_Sit_Right_Down_and_Write_Myself_a_Letter.

Bibliography

Baum, L. Frank. *Tin Woodman of Oz*. SeaWolf Press, 2019.

Carnegie, Dale. *How to Win Friends and Influence People*. New York: Simon & Schuster, 1936.

Chabris, Christopher, and Daniel Simons. *The Invisible Gorilla: And Other Ways Our Intuitions Deceive Us*. New York: Harmony Books, 2011.

Chapman, Gary. *The Five Love Languages: The Secret to Love That Lasts*. Chicago: Northfield Pub, 2010.

Covey, Stephen. *The 7 Habits of Highly Effective People: Powerful Lessons in Personal Change*. New York: Free Press, 2004.

Eiseley, Loren. *The Star Thrower*. New York: Harcourt Brace & Company, 1979.

Henry, O. *O. Henry: The Complete Works*. Pandora's Box. Kindle edition, 2020.

Hines, Kevin. *Cracked, Not Broken: Surviving and Thriving After a Suicide Attempt*. Maryland: Rowman & Littlefield, 2013.

Hugo, Victor. *Les Misérables*, 1862.

Parkinson, Cyril Northcote. *Parkinson's Law and Other Studies in Administration*. Houghton Mifflin, 1957.

About The Author

Steve Fales describes himself as an ordinary guy with a desire to have a positive effect on everyone he meets. He sees the great void of practical love and does his best to fill it. He and his wife Linda, who were married in their early twenties, live in south Florida and have two grown daughters.

Steve is the founder of several small businesses. He is a marathon runner, triathlete, life-long learner, and an avid chess player.

Through writing, presentations, corporate consulting, and individual coaching, Steve communicates principles and techniques for personal and professional development and biblical spiritual growth. For information on these services and to read more of his writings, visit: twentythousandfeet.com.

Steve's life mission is to leave a legacy of having achieved his full potential and helping others do the same.

Also by Steve Fales:

Companality: Developing Intentional Organizational Culture

Three Years Of Tuesday Mornings: 156 e-mails about business and life